Philosophy of Science: A Very Short Introduction

VERY SHORT INTRODUCTIONS are for anyone wanting a stimulating and accessible way in to a new subject. They are written by experts, and have been published in more than 25 languages worldwide.

The series began in 1995, and now represents a wide variety of topics in history, philosophy, religion, science, and the humanities. Over the next few years it will grow to a library of around 200 volumes – a Very Short Introduction to everything from ancient Egypt and Indian philosophy to conceptual art and cosmology.

Very Short Introductions available now:

Available soon:

For more information visit our web site

www.oup.co.uk/vsi

Samir Okasha

PHILOSOPHY OF SCIENCE

A Very Short Introduction

OXFORD
UNIVERSITY PRESS

OXFORD
UNIVERSITY PRESS

Great Clarendon Street, Oxford OX2 6DP

Oxford University Press is a department of the University of Oxford.
It furthers the University's objective of excellence in research, scholarship,
and education by publishing worldwide in

Oxford New York

Auckland Bangkok Buenos Aires Cape Town Chennai
Dar es Salaam Delhi Hong Kong Istanbul Karachi Kolkata
Kuala Lumpur Madrid Melbourne Mexico City Mumbai Nairobi
São Paulo Shanghai Taipei Tokyo Toronto

Oxford is a registered trade mark of Oxford University Press
in the UK and in certain other countries

Published in the United States
by Oxford University Press Inc., New York

British Library Cataloguing in Publication Data

Data available

Library of Congress Cataloging in Publication Data

Data available

ISBN 978-0-19-280283-5

11 13 15 17 19 20 18 16 14 12

Typeset by RefineCatch Ltd, Bungay, Suffolk
Printed in Great Britain by
Ashford Colour Press Ltd, Gosport, Hampshire

Contents

Acknowledgements

I would like to thank Bill Newton-Smith, Peter Lipton, Elizabeth Okasha, Liz Richardson and Shelley Cox for reading and commenting on earlier versions of this material.

Samir Okasha

List of illustrations

The publisher and the author apologize for any errors or omissions in the above list. If contacted they will be pleased to rectify these at the earliest opportunity.

Chapter 1
What is science?

What is science? This question may seem easy to answer: everybody knows that subjects such as physics, chemistry, and biology constitute science, while subjects such as art, music, and theology do not. But when as philosophers we ask what science is, that is not the sort of answer we want. We are not asking for a mere list of the activities that are usually called 'science'. Rather, we are asking what common feature all the things on that list share, i.e. what it is that *makes* something a science. Understood this way, our question is not so trivial.

But you may still think the question is relatively straightforward. Surely science is just the attempt to understand, explain, and predict the world we live in? This is certainly a reasonable answer. But is it the whole story? After all, the various religions also attempt to understand and explain the world, but religion is not usually regarded as a branch of science. Similarly, astrology and fortune-telling are attempts to predict the future, but most people would not describe these activities as science. Or consider history. Historians try to understand and explain what happened in the past, but history is usually classified as an arts subject not a science subject. As with many philosophical questions, the question 'what is science?' turns out to be trickier than it looks at first sight.

Many people believe that the distinguishing features of science lie in the particular methods scientists use to investigate the world. This suggestion is quite plausible. For many sciences do employ distinctive methods of enquiry that are not found in non-scientific disciplines. An obvious example is the use of experiments, which historically marks a turning-point in the development of modern science. Not all the sciences are experimental though – astronomers obviously cannot do experiments on the heavens, but have to content themselves with careful observation instead. The same is true of many social sciences. Another important feature of science is the construction of theories. Scientists do not simply record the results of experiment and observation in a log book – they usually want to explain those results in terms of a general theory. This is not always easy to do, but there have been some striking successes. One of the key problems in philosophy of science is to understand how techniques such as experimentation, observation, and theory-construction have enabled scientists to unravel so many of nature's secrets.

The origins of modern science

In today's schools and universities, science is taught in a largely ahistorical way. Textbooks present the key ideas of a scientific discipline in as convenient a form as possible, with little mention of the lengthy and often tortuous historical process that led to their discovery. As a pedagogical strategy, this makes good sense. But some appreciation of the history of scientific ideas is helpful for understanding the issues that interest philosophers of science. Indeed as we shall see in Chapter 5, it has been argued that close attention to the history of science is indispensable for doing good philosophy of science.

The origins of modern science lie in a period of rapid scientific development that occurred in Europe between the years 1500 and 1750, which we now refer to as the scientific revolution. Of course scientific investigations were pursued in ancient and medieval times too – the scientific revolution did not come from nowhere. In these earlier periods the dominant world-view was Aristotelianism, named after the ancient Greek philosopher Aristotle, who put forward detailed theories in physics, biology, astronomy, and cosmology. But Aristotle's ideas would seem very strange to a modern scientist, as would his methods of enquiry. To pick just one example, he believed that all earthly bodies are composed of just four elements: earth, fire, air, and water. This view is obviously at odds with what modern chemistry tells us.

The first crucial step in the development of the modern scientific world-view was the Copernican revolution. In 1542 the Polish astronomer Nicolas Copernicus (1473–1543) published a book attacking the geocentric model of the universe, which placed the stationary earth at the centre of the universe with the planets and the sun in orbit around it. Geocentric astronomy, also known as Ptolemaic astronomy after the ancient Greek astronomer Ptolemy, lay at the heart of the Aristotelian world-view, and had gone largely unchallenged for 1,800 years. But Copernicus suggested an alternative: the *sun* was the fixed centre of the universe, and the planets, including the earth, were in orbit around the sun (Figure 1). On this heliocentric model the earth is regarded as just another planet, and so loses the unique status that tradition had accorded it. Copernicus' theory initially met with much resistance, not least from the Catholic Church who regarded it as contravening the Scriptures and in 1616 banned books advocating the earth's motion. But within 100 years Copernicanism had become established scientific orthodoxy.

Copernicus' innovation did not merely lead to a better astronomy. Indirectly, it led to the development of modern physics, through the work of Johannes Kepler (1571–1630) and Galileo Galilei (1564–1642). Kepler discovered that the planets do not move in circular orbits around the sun, as Copernicus thought, but rather in ellipses. This was his crucial 'first law' of planetary motion; his second and third laws specify the speeds at which the planets orbit the sun.

1. Copernicus' heliocentric model of the universe, showing the planets, including the earth, orbiting the sun.

Taken together, Kepler's laws provided a far superior planetary theory than had ever been advanced before, solving problems that had confounded astronomers for centuries. Galileo was a life-long supporter of Copernicanism, and one of the early pioneers of the telescope. When he pointed his telescope at the heavens, he made a wealth of amazing discoveries, including mountains on the moon, a vast array of stars, sun-spots, and Jupiter's moons. All of these conflicted thoroughly with Aristotelian cosmology, and played a pivotal role in converting the scientific community to Copernicanism.

Galileo's most enduring contribution, however, lay not in astronomy but in mechanics, where he refuted the Aristotelian theory that heavier bodies fall faster than lighter ones. In place of this theory, Galileo made the counter-intuitive suggestion that all

4

freely falling bodies will fall towards the earth at the same rate, irrespective of their weight (Figure 2). (Of course in practice, if you drop a feather and a cannon-ball from the same height the cannon-ball will land first, but Galileo argued that this is simply due to air resistance – in a vacuum, they would land together.) Furthermore, he argued that freely falling bodies accelerate uniformly, i.e. gain equal increments of speed in equal times; this is known as Galileo's law of free-fall. Galileo provided persuasive though not totally conclusive evidence for this law, which formed the centrepiece of his theory of mechanics.

Galileo is generally regarded as the first truly modern physicist. He was the first to show that the language of mathematics could be used to describe the behaviour of actual objects in the material world, such as falling bodies, projectiles, etc. To us this seems obvious – today's scientific theories are routinely formulated in mathematical language, not only in the physical sciences but also in biology and economics. But in Galileo's day it was not obvious: mathematics was widely regarded as dealing with purely abstract entities, and hence inapplicable to physical reality. Another innovative aspect of Galileo's work was his emphasis on the importance of testing hypotheses experimentally. To the modern scientist, this may again seem obvious. But at the time that Galileo was working, experimentation was not generally regarded as a reliable means of gaining knowledge. Galileo's emphasis on experimental testing marks the beginning of an empirical approach to studying nature that continues to this day.

The period following Galileo's death saw the scientific revolution rapidly gain in momentum. The French philosopher, mathematician, and scientist René Descartes (1596–1650) developed a radical new 'mechanical philosophy', according to which the physical world consists simply of inert particles of matter interacting and colliding with one another. The laws governing the motion of these particles or 'corpuscles' held the key to understanding the structure of the Copernican universe, Descartes

'They were seen to fall evenly.'

2. Sketch of Galileo's mythical experiment on the velocity of objects dropped from the Leaning Tower of Pisa.

believed. The mechanical philosophy promised to explain all observable phenomena in terms of the motion of these inert, insensible corpuscles, and quickly became the dominant scientific vision of the second half of the 17th century; to some extent it is still with us today. Versions of the mechanical philosophy were espoused by figures such as Huygens, Gassendi, Hooke, Boyle, and others; its widespread acceptance marked the final downfall of the Aristotelian world-view.

The scientific revolution culminated in the work of Isaac Newton (1643–1727), whose achievements stand unparalleled in the history of science. Newton's masterpiece was his *Mathematical Principles of Natural Philosophy*, published in 1687. Newton agreed with the mechanical philosophers that the universe consists simply of particles in motion, but sought to improve on Descartes' laws of motion and rules of collision. The result was a dynamical and mechanical theory of great power, based around Newton's three laws of motion and his famous principle of universal gravitation. According to this principle, every body in the universe exerts a gravitational attraction on every other body; the strength of the attraction between two bodies depends on the product of their masses, and on the distance between them squared. The laws of motion then specify how this gravitational force affects the bodies' motions. Newton elaborated his theory with great mathematical precision and rigour, inventing the mathematical technique we now call 'calculus'. Strikingly, Newton was able to show that Kepler's laws of planetary motion and Galileo's law of free-fall (both with certain minor modifications) were logical consequences of his laws of motion and gravitation. In other words, the very same laws would explain the motions of bodies in both terrestrial and celestial domains, and were formulated by Newton in a precise quantitative form.

Newtonian physics provided the framework for science for the next 200 years or so, quickly replacing Cartesian physics. Scientific confidence grew rapidly in this period, due largely to the success of

Newton's theory, which was widely believed to have revealed the true workings of nature, and to be capable of explaining everything, in principle at least. Detailed attempts were made to extend the Newtonian mode of explanation to more and more phenomena. The 18th and 19th centuries both saw notable scientific advances, particularly in the study of chemistry, optics, energy, thermodynamics, and electromagnetism. But for the most part, these developments were regarded as falling within a broadly Newtonian conception of the universe. Scientists accepted Newton's conception as essentially correct; all that remained to be done was to fill in the details.

Confidence in the Newtonian picture was shattered in the early years of the 20th century, thanks to two revolutionary new developments in physics: relativity theory and quantum mechanics. Relativity theory, discovered by Einstein, showed that Newtonian mechanics does not give the right results when applied to very massive objects, or objects moving at very high velocities. Quantum mechanics, conversely, shows that the Newtonian theory does not work when applied on a very small scale, to subatomic particles. Both relativity theory and quantum mechanics, especially the latter, are very strange and radical theories, making claims about the nature of reality that many people find hard to accept or even understand. Their emergence caused considerable conceptual upheaval in physics, which continues to this day.

So far our brief account of the history of science has focused mainly on physics. This is no accident, as physics is both historically very important and in a sense the most fundamental of all scientific disciplines. For the objects that other sciences study are themselves made up of physical entities. Consider botany, for example. Botanists study plants, which are ultimately composed of molecules and atoms, which are physical particles. So botany is obviously less fundamental than physics – though that is not to say it is any less important. This is a point we shall return to in Chapter 3. But even a brief description of modern science's origins would be incomplete if it omitted all mention of the non-physical sciences.

In biology, the event that stands out is Charles Darwin's discovery of the theory of evolution by natural selection, published in *The Origin of Species* in 1859. Until then it was widely believed that the different species had been separately created by God, as the Book of Genesis teaches. But Darwin argued that contemporary species have actually evolved from ancestral ones, through a process known as natural selection. Natural selection occurs when some organisms leave more offspring than others, depending on their physical characteristics; if these characteristics are then inherited by their offspring, over time the population will become better and better adapted to the environment. Simple though this process is, over a large number of generations it can cause one species to evolve into a wholly new one, Darwin argued. So persuasive was the evidence Darwin adduced for his theory that by the start of the 20th century it was accepted as scientific orthodoxy, despite considerable theological opposition (Figure 3). Subsequent work has provided striking confirmation of Darwin's theory, which forms the centrepiece of the modern biological world view.

The 20th century witnessed another revolution in biology that is not yet complete: the emergence of molecular biology, in particular molecular genetics. In 1953 Watson and Crick discovered the structure of DNA, the hereditary material that makes up the genes in the cells of living creatures (Figure 4). Watson and Crick's discovery explained how genetic information can be copied from one cell to another, and thus passed down from parent to offspring, thereby explaining why offspring tend to resemble their parents. Their discovery opened up an exciting new area of biological research. In the 50 years since Watson and Crick's work, molecular biology has grown fast, transforming our understanding of heredity and of how genes build organisms. The recent attempt to provide a molecular-level description of the complete set of genes in a human

MR. BERGH TO THE RESCUE.

THE DEFRAUDED GORILLA. "That *Man* wants to claim my Pedigree. He says he is one of my Descendants."

Mr. BERGH. "Now, Mr. DARWIN, how could you insult him so?"

3. Darwin's suggestion that humans and apes have descended from common ancestors caused consternation in Victorian England.

being, known as the Human Genome Project, is an indication of how far molecular biology has come. The 21st century will see further exciting developments in this field.

More resources have been devoted to scientific research in the last hundred years than ever before. One result has been an explosion of new scientific disciplines, such as computer science, artificial intelligence, linguistics, and neuroscience. Possibly the most significant event of the last 30 years is the rise of cognitive science,

4. James Watson and Francis Crick with the famous 'double helix' their molecular model of the structure of DNA, discovered in 1953.

which studies various aspects of human cognition such as perception, memory, learning, and reasoning, and has transformed traditional psychology. Much of the impetus for cognitive science comes from the idea that the human mind is in some respects similar to a computer, and thus that human mental processes can be understood by comparing them to the operations computers carry out. Cognitive science is still in its infancy, but promises to reveal much about the workings of the mind. The social sciences, especially economics and sociology, have also flourished in the 20th century, though many people believe they still lag behind the natural sciences in terms of sophistication and rigour. This is an issue we shall return to in Chapter 7.

What is philosophy of science?

The principal task of philosophy of science is to analyse the methods of enquiry used in the various sciences. You may wonder why this task should fall to philosophers, rather than to the scientists themselves. This is a good question. Part of the answer is that looking at science from a philosophical perspective allows us to probe deeper – to uncover assumptions that are implicit in scientific practice, but which scientists do not explicitly discuss. To illustrate, consider scientific experimentation. Suppose a scientist does an experiment and gets a particular result. He repeats the experiment a few times and keeps getting the same result. After that he will probably stop, confident that were he to keep repeating the experiment, under exactly the same conditions, he would continue to get the same result. This assumption may seem obvious, but as philosophers we want to question it. *Why* assume that future repetitions of the experiment will yield the same result? How do we know this is true? The scientist is unlikely to spend too much time puzzling over these somewhat curious questions: he probably has better things to do. They are quintessentially philosophical questions, to which we return in the next chapter.

So part of the job of philosophy of science is to question assumptions that scientists take for granted. But it would be wrong to imply that scientists never discuss philosophical issues themselves. Indeed, historically, many scientists have played an important role in the development of philosophy of science. Descartes, Newton, and Einstein are prominent examples. Each was deeply interested in philosophical questions about how science should proceed, what methods of enquiry it should use, how much confidence we should place in those methods, whether there are limits to scientific knowledge, and so on. As we shall see, these questions still lie at the heart of contemporary philosophy of science. So the issues that interest philosophers of science are not 'merely philosophical'; on the contrary, they have engaged the attention of some of the greatest scientists of all. That having been said, it must be admitted that many scientists today take little interest in philosophy of science, and know little about it. While this is unfortunate, it is not an indication that philosophical issues are no longer relevant. Rather, it is a consequence of the increasingly specialized nature of science, and of the polarization between the sciences and the humanities that characterizes the modern education system.

You may still be wondering exactly what philosophy of science is all about. For to say that it 'studies the methods of science', as we did above, is not really to say very much. Rather than try to provide a more informative definition, we will proceed straight to consider a typical problem in the philosophy of science.

Science and pseudo-science

Recall the question with which we began: what is science? Karl Popper, an influential 20th-century philosopher of science, thought that the fundamental feature of a scientific theory is that it should be falsifiable. To call a theory falsifiable is not to say that it is false. Rather, it means that the theory makes some definite predictions that are capable of being tested against experience. If these predictions turn out to be wrong, then the theory has been falsified, or disproved. So a falsifiable theory is one that we might discover to be false – it is not compatible with every possible course of experience. Popper thought that some supposedly scientific theories did not satisfy this condition and thus did not deserve to be called science at all; rather they were merely pseudo-science.

Freud's psychoanalytic theory was one of Popper's favourite examples of pseudo-science. According to Popper, Freud's theory could be reconciled with any empirical findings whatsoever. Whatever a patient's behaviour, Freudians could find an explanation of it in terms of their theory – they would never admit that their theory was wrong. Popper illustrated his point with the following example. Imagine a man who pushes a child into a river with the intention of murdering him, and another man who sacrifices his life in order to save the child. Freudians can explain both men's behaviour with equal ease: the first was repressed, and the second had achieved sublimation. Popper argued that through the use of such concepts as repression, sublimation, and unconscious desires, Freud's theory could be rendered compatible with any clinical data whatever; it was thus unfalsifiable.

The same was true of Marx's theory of history, Popper maintained. Marx claimed that in industrialized societies around the world, capitalism would give way to socialism and ultimately to communism. But when this didn't happen, instead of admitting that Marx's theory was wrong, Marxists would invent an *ad hoc* explanation for why what happened was actually perfectly consistent with their theory. For example, they might say that the inevitable progress to communism had been temporarily slowed by the rise of the welfare state, which 'softened' the proletariat and weakened their revolutionary zeal. In this sort of way, Marx's theory could be made compatible with any possible course of events, just like Freud's. Therefore neither theory qualifies as genuinely scientific, according to Popper's criterion.

Popper contrasted Freud's and Marx's theories with Einstein's theory of gravitation, also known as general relativity. Unlike Freud's and Marx's theories, Einstein's theory made a very definite prediction: that light rays from distant stars would be deflected by the gravitational field of the sun. Normally this effect would be impossible to observe – except during a solar eclipse. In 1919 the English astrophysicist Sir Arthur Eddington organized two expeditions to observe the solar eclipse of that year, one to Brazil and one to the island of Principe off the Atlantic coast of Africa, with the aim of testing Einstein's prediction. The expeditions found that starlight was indeed deflected by the sun, by almost exactly the amount Einstein had predicted. Popper was very impressed by this. Einstein's theory had made a definite, precise prediction, which was confirmed by observations. Had it turned out that starlight was not deflected by the sun, this would have showed that Einstein was wrong. So Einstein's theory satisfies the criterion of falsifiability.

Popper's attempt to demarcate science from pseudo-science is intuitively quite plausible. There is certainly something fishy about a theory that can be made to fit any empirical data whatsoever. But some philosophers regard Popper's criterion as overly simplistic. Popper criticized Freudians and Marxists for explaining away any data that appeared to conflict with their theories, rather than accepting that the theories had been refuted. This certainly looks like a suspicious procedure. However, there is some evidence that this very procedure is routinely used by 'respectable' scientists – whom Popper would not want to accuse of engaging in pseudo-science – and has led to important scientific discoveries.

Another astronomical example can illustrate this. Newton's gravitational theory, which we encountered earlier, made predictions about the paths the planets should follow as they orbit the sun. For the most part, these predictions were borne out by observation. However, the observed orbit of Uranus consistently differed from what Newton's theory predicted. This puzzle was solved in 1846 by two scientists, Adams in England and Leverrier in France, working independently. They suggested that there was another planet, as yet undiscovered, exerting an additional gravitational force on Uranus. Adams and Leverrier were able to calculate the mass and position that this planet would have to have, if its gravitational pull was indeed responsible for Uranus' strange behaviour. Shortly afterwards the planet Neptune was discovered, almost exactly where Adams and Leverrier had predicted.

Now clearly we should not criticize Adams' and Leverrier's behaviour as 'unscientific' – after all, it led to the discovery of a new planet. But they did precisely what Popper criticized the Marxists for doing. They began with a theory – Newton's theory of gravity – which made an incorrect prediction about Uranus' orbit. Rather than concluding that Newton's theory must be wrong, they stuck by

15

the theory and attempted to explain away the conflicting observations by postulating a new planet. Similarly, when capitalism showed no signs of giving way to communism, Marxists did not conclude that Marx's theory must be wrong, but stuck by the theory and tried to explain away the conflicting observations in other ways. So surely it is unfair to accuse Marxists of engaging in pseudo-science if we allow that what Adams and Leverrier did counted as good, indeed exemplary, science?

This suggests that Popper's attempt to demarcate science from pseudo-science cannot be quite right, despite its initial plausibility. For the Adams/Leverrier example is by no means atypical. In general, scientists do not just abandon their theories whenever they conflict with the observational data. Usually they look for ways of eliminating the conflict without having to give up their theory; this is a point we shall return to in Chapter 5. And it is worth remembering that virtually every theory in science conflicts with some observations – finding a theory that fits all the data perfectly is extremely difficult. Obviously if a theory persistently conflicts with more and more data, and no plausible ways of explaining away the conflict are found, it will eventually have to be rejected. But little progress would be made if scientists simply abandoned their theories at the first sign of trouble.

The failure of Popper's demarcation criterion throws up an important question. Is it actually possible to find some common feature shared by all the things we call 'science', and not shared by anything else? Popper assumed that the answer to this question was yes. He felt that Freud's and Marx's theories were clearly unscientific, so there must be some feature that they lack and that genuine scientific theories possess. But whether or not we accept Popper's negative assessment of Freud and Marx, his assumption that science has an 'essential nature' is questionable. After all, science is a heterogeneous activity, encompassing a wide range of different disciplines and theories. It may be that they share some fixed set of features that define what it is to be a science, but it may

16

not. The philosopher Ludwig Wittgenstein argued that there is no fixed set of features that define what it is to be a 'game'. Rather, there is a loose cluster of features most of which are possessed by most games. But any particular game may lack any of the features in the cluster and still be a game. The same may be true of science. If so, a simple criterion for demarcating science from pseudo-science is unlikely to be found.

Chapter 2
Scientific reasoning

Scientists often tell us things about the world that we would not otherwise have believed. For example, biologists tell us that we are closely related to chimpanzees, geologists tell us that Africa and South America used to be joined together, and cosmologists tell us that the universe is expanding. But how did scientists reach these unlikely-sounding conclusions? After all, no one has ever seen one species evolve from another, or a single continent split into two, or the universe getting bigger. The answer, of course, is that scientists arrived at these beliefs by a process of reasoning or inference. But it would be nice to know more about this process. What exactly is the nature of scientific reasoning? And how much confidence should we place in the inferences scientists make? These are the topics of this chapter.

Deduction and induction

Logicians make an important distinction between deductive and inductive patterns of reasoning. An example of a piece of deductive reasoning, or a deductive inference, is the following:

All Frenchmen like red wine
Pierre is a Frenchman

Therefore, Pierre likes red wine

The first two statements are called the premises of the inference, while the third statement is called the conclusion. This is a deductive inference because it has the following property: if the premises are true, then the conclusion must be true too. In other words, if it's true that all Frenchman like red wine, and if it's true that Pierre is a Frenchman, it follows that Pierre does indeed like red wine. This is sometimes expressed by saying that the premises of the inference entail the conclusion. Of course, the premises of this inference are almost certainly not true – there are bound to be Frenchmen who do not like red wine. But that is not the point. What makes the inference deductive is the existence of an appropriate relation between premises and conclusion, namely that if the premises are true, the conclusion must be true too. Whether the premises are actually true is a different matter, which doesn't affect the status of the inference as deductive.

Not all inferences are deductive. Consider the following example:

The first five eggs in the box were rotten
All the eggs have the same best-before date stamped on them

Therefore, the sixth egg will be rotten too

This looks like a perfectly sensible piece of reasoning. But nonetheless it is not deductive, for the premises do not entail the conclusion. Even if the first five eggs were indeed rotten, and even if all the eggs do have the same best-before date stamped on them, this does not guarantee that the sixth egg will be rotten too. It is quite conceivable that the sixth egg will be perfectly good. In other words, it is logically possible for the premises of this inference to be true and yet the conclusion false, so the inference is not deductive. Instead it is known as an inductive inference. In inductive inference, or inductive reasoning, we move from premises about objects we have examined to conclusions about objects we haven't examined – in this example, eggs.

Deductive reasoning is a much safer activity than inductive reasoning. When we reason deductively, we can be certain that if we start with true premises, we will end up with a true conclusion. But the same does not hold for inductive reasoning. On the contrary, inductive reasoning is quite capable of taking us from true premises to a false conclusion. Despite this defect, we seem to rely on inductive reasoning throughout our lives, often without even thinking about it. For example, when you turn on your computer in the morning, you are confident it will not explode in your face. Why? Because you turn on your computer every morning, and it has never exploded in your face up to now. But the inference from 'up until now, my computer has not exploded when I turned it on' to 'my computer will not explode when I turn it on this time' is inductive, not deductive. The premiss of this inference does not entail the conclusion. It is logically possible that your computer will explode this time, even though it has never done so previously.

Other examples of inductive reasoning in everyday life can readily be found. When you turn the steering wheel of your car anticlockwise, you assume the car will go to the left not the right. Whenever you drive in traffic, you effectively stake your life on this assumption. But what makes you so sure that it's true? If someone asked you to justify your conviction, what would you say? Unless you are a mechanic, you would probably reply: 'every time I've turned the steering wheel anticlockwise in the past, the car has gone to the left. Therefore, the same will happen when I turn the steering wheel anticlockwise this time.' Again, this is an inductive inference, not a deductive one. Reasoning inductively seems to be an indispensable part of everyday life.

Do scientists use inductive reasoning too? The answer seems to be yes. Consider the genetic disease known as Down's syndrome (DS for short). Geneticists tell us that DS sufferers have an additional chromosome – they have 47 instead of the normal 46 (Figure 5). How do they know this? The answer, of course, is that they

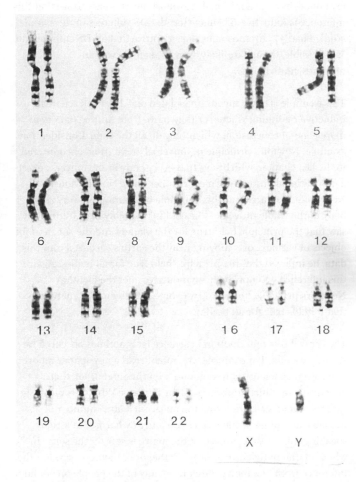

5. A representation of the complete set of chromosomes – or karyotype – of a person with Down's syndrome. There are three copies of chromosome 21, as opposed to the two copies most people have, giving 47 chromosomes in total.

examined a large number of DS sufferers and found that each had an additional chromosome. They then reasoned inductively to the conclusion that all DS sufferers, including ones they hadn't examined, have an additional chromosome. It is easy to see that this inference is inductive. The fact that the DS sufferers in the sample studied had 47 chromosomes doesn't prove that all DS sufferers do. It is possible, though unlikely, that the sample was an unrepresentative one.

This example is by no means an isolated one. In effect, scientists use inductive reasoning whenever they move from limited data to a more general conclusion, which they do all the time. Consider, for example, Newton's principle of universal gravitation, encountered in the last chapter, which says that every body in the universe exerts a gravitational attraction on every other body. Now obviously, Newton did not arrive at this principle by examining every single body in the whole universe – he couldn't possibly have. Rather, he saw that the principle held true for the planets and the sun, and for objects of various sorts moving near the earth's surface. From this data, he inferred that the principle held true for all bodies. Again, this inference was obviously an inductive one: the fact that Newton's principle holds true for some bodies doesn't guarantee that it holds true for all bodies.

The central role of induction in science is sometimes obscured by the way we talk. For example, you might read a newspaper report that says that scientists have found 'experimental proof' that genetically modified maize is safe for humans. What this means is that the scientists have tested the maize on a large number of humans, and none of them have come to any harm. But strictly speaking this doesn't *prove* that the maize is safe, in the sense in which mathematicians can prove Pythagoras' theorem, say. For the inference from 'the maize didn't harm any of the people on whom it was tested' to 'the maize will not harm anyone' is inductive, not deductive. The newspaper report should really have said that scientists have found extremely good *evidence* that the maize is safe for humans. The word 'proof' should strictly only be used when we are dealing with deductive inferences. In this strict sense of the word, scientific hypotheses can rarely, if ever, be proved true by the data.

Most philosophers think it's obvious that science relies heavily on inductive reasoning, indeed so obvious that it hardly needs arguing for. But, remarkably, this was denied by the philosopher Karl Popper, who we met in the last chapter. Popper claimed that scientists only need to use deductive inferences. This would be nice if it were true, for deductive inferences are much safer than inductive ones, as we have seen.

Popper's basic argument was this. Although it is not possible to prove that a scientific theory is true from a limited data sample, it is possible to prove that a theory is false. Suppose a scientist is considering the theory that all pieces of metal conduct electricity. Even if every piece of metal she examines does conduct electricity, this doesn't prove that the theory is true, for reasons that we've seen. But if she finds even one piece of metal that does not conduct electricity, this does prove that the theory is false. For the inference from 'this piece of metal does not conduct electricity' to 'it is false that all pieces of metal conduct electricity' is a deductive inference – the premiss entails the conclusion. So if a scientist is only interested in demonstrating that a given theory is false, she may be able to accomplish her goal without the use of inductive inferences.

The weakness of Popper's argument is obvious. For scientists are not only interested in showing that certain theories are false. When a scientist collects experimental data, her aim might be to show that a particular theory – her arch-rival's theory perhaps – is false. But much more likely, she is trying to convince people that her own theory is true. And in order to do that, she will have to resort to inductive reasoning of some sort. So Popper's attempt to show that science can get by without induction does not succeed.

Hume's problem

Although inductive reasoning is not logically watertight, it nonetheless seems like a perfectly sensible way of forming beliefs about the world. The fact that the sun has risen every day up until now may not prove that it will rise tomorrow, but surely it gives us very good reason to think it will? If you came across someone who professed to be entirely agnostic about whether the sun will rise tomorrow or not, you would regard them as very strange indeed, if not irrational.

But what justifies this faith we place in induction? How should we go about persuading someone who refuses to reason inductively that they are wrong? The 18th-century Scottish philosopher David Hume (1711–1776) gave a simple but radical answer to this question. He argued that the use of induction cannot be rationally justified at all. Hume admitted that we use induction all the time, in everyday life and in science, but he insisted this was just a matter of brute animal habit. If challenged to provide a good reason for using induction, we can give no satisfactory answer, he thought.

How did Hume arrive at this startling conclusion? He began by noting that whenever we make inductive inferences, we seem to presuppose what he called the 'uniformity of nature' (UN). To see what Hume means by this, recall some of the inductive inferences from the last section. We had the inference from 'my computer hasn't exploded up to now' to 'my computer won't explode today'; from 'all examined DS sufferers have an extra chromosome' to 'all DS sufferers have an extra chromosome'; from 'all bodies observed so far obey Newton's law of gravity' to 'all bodies obey Newton's law of gravity'; and so on. In each of these cases, our reasoning seems to depend on the assumption that objects we haven't examined will be similar, in the relevant respects, to objects of the same sort that we have examined. That assumption is what Hume means by the uniformity of nature.

But how do we know that the UN assumption is actually true, Hume asks? Can we perhaps prove its truth somehow (in the strict sense of proof)? No, says Hume, we cannot. For it is easy to imagine a universe where nature is not uniform, but changes its course randomly from day to day. In such a universe, computers might sometimes explode for no reason, water might sometimes intoxicate us without warning, billiard balls might sometimes stop dead on colliding, and so on. Since such a 'non-uniform' universe is conceivable, it follows that we cannot strictly prove the truth of UN. For if we could prove that UN is true, then the non-uniform universe would be a logical impossibility.

Granted that we cannot prove UN, we might nonetheless hope to find good empirical evidence for its truth. After all, since UN has always held true up to now, surely that gives us good reason for thinking it is true? But this argument begs the question, says Hume! For it is itself an inductive argument, and so itself depends on the UN assumption. An argument that assumes UN from the outset clearly cannot be used to show that UN is true. To put the point another way, it is certainly an established fact that nature has behaved largely uniformly up to now. But we cannot appeal to this fact to argue that nature will continue to be uniform, because this assumes that what has happened in the past is a reliable guide to what will happen in the future – which *is* the uniformity of nature assumption. If we try to argue for UN on empirical grounds, we end up reasoning in a circle.

The force of Hume's point can be appreciated by imagining how you would go about persuading someone who doesn't trust inductive reasoning that they should. You would probably say: 'look, inductive reasoning has worked pretty well up until now. By using induction scientists have split the atom, landed men on the moon, invented computers, and so on. Whereas people who haven't used induction have tended to die nasty deaths. They have eaten arsenic believing that it would nourish them, jumped off tall buildings believing that they would fly, and so on (Figure 6). Therefore it will clearly pay you

25

6. What happens to people who don't trust induction.

to reason inductively.' But of course this wouldn't convince the doubter. For to argue that induction is trustworthy because it has worked well up to now is to reason in an inductive way. Such an argument would carry no weight with someone who doesn't already trust induction. That is Hume's fundamental point.

So the position is this. Hume points out that our inductive inferences rest on the UN assumption. But we cannot prove that UN is true, and we cannot produce empirical evidence for its truth without begging the question. So our inductive inferences rest on an assumption about the world for which we have no good grounds. Hume concludes that our confidence in induction is just blind faith – it admits of no rational justification whatever.

This intriguing argument has exerted a powerful influence on the philosophy of science, and continues to do so today. (Popper's unsuccessful attempt to show that scientists need only use deductive inferences was motivated by his belief that Hume had shown the total irrationality of inductive reasoning.) The influence of Hume's argument is not hard to understand. For normally we think of science as the very paradigm of rational enquiry. We place great faith in what scientists tell us about the world. Every time we travel by aeroplane, we put our lives in the hands of the scientists who designed the plane. But science relies on induction, and Hume's argument seems to show that induction cannot be rationally justified. If Hume is right, the foundations on which science is built do not look quite as solid as we might have hoped. This puzzling state of affairs is known as Hume's problem of induction.

Philosophers have responded to Hume's problem in literally dozens of different ways; this is still an active area of research today. Some people believe the key lies in the concept of probability. This suggestion is quite plausible. For it is natural to think that although the premises of an inductive inference do not guarantee the truth of the conclusion, they do make it quite probable. So even if scientific knowledge cannot be certain, it may nonetheless be highly probable. But this response to Hume's problem generates difficulties of its own, and is by no means universally accepted; we will return to it in due course.

Another popular response is to admit that induction cannot be rationally justified, but to argue that this is not really so problematic after all. How might one defend such a position? Some philosophers have argued that induction is so fundamental to how we think and reason that it's not the sort of thing that could be justified. Peter Strawson, an influential contemporary philosopher, defended this view with the following analogy. If someone worried about whether a particular action was legal, they could consult the law-books and compare the action with what the law-books say. But suppose someone worried about whether the law itself was legal. This is an odd worry indeed. For the law is the standard against which the legality of other things is judged, and it makes little sense to enquire whether the standard itself is legal. The same applies to induction, Strawson argued. Induction is one of the standards we use to decide whether claims about the world are justified. For example, we use induction to judge whether a pharmaceutical company's claim about the amazing benefits of its new drug are justified. So it makes little sense to ask whether induction itself is justified.

Has Strawson really succeeded in defusing Hume's problem? Some philosophers say yes, others say no. But most people agree that it is very hard to see how there could be a satisfactory justification of induction. (Frank Ramsey, a Cambridge philosopher from the 1920s, said that to ask for a justification of induction was 'to cry for the moon'.) Whether this is something that should worry us, or shake our faith in science, is a difficult question that you should ponder for yourself.

Inference to the best explanation

The inductive inferences we've examined so far have all had
essentially the same structure. In each case, the premiss of the
inference has had the form 'all x's examined so far have been y',
and the conclusion has had the form 'the next x to be examined
will be y', or sometimes, 'all x's are y'. In other words, these
inferences take us from examined to unexamined instances of a
given kind.

Such inferences are widely used in everyday life and in science, as
we have seen. However, there is another common type of non-
deductive inference that doesn't fit this simple pattern. Consider the
following example:

The cheese in the larder has disappeared, apart from a
few crumbs
Scratching noises were heard coming from the larder last night

---

Therefore, the cheese was eaten by a mouse

It is obvious that this inference is non-deductive: the premisses do
not entail the conclusion. For the cheese could have been stolen
by the maid, who cleverly left a few crumbs to make it look like
the handiwork of a mouse (Figure 7). And the scratching noises
could have been caused in any number of ways – perhaps they
were due to the boiler overheating. Nonetheless, the inference is
clearly a reasonable one. For the hypothesis that a mouse ate the
cheese seems to provide a better explanation of the data than do
the various alternative explanations. After all, maids do not
normally steal cheese, and modern boilers do not tend to
overheat. Whereas mice do normally eat cheese when they get the
chance, and do tend to make scratching sounds. So although we
cannot be certain that the mouse hypothesis is true, on balance it
looks quite plausible: it is the best way of accounting for the
available data.

7. The mouse hypothesis and the maid hypothesis can both account for the missing cheese.

Reasoning of this sort is known as 'inference to the best explanation', for obvious reasons, or IBE for short. Certain terminological confusions surround the relation between IBE and induction. Some philosophers describe IBE as a type of inductive inference; in effect, they use 'inductive inference' to mean 'any inference which is not deductive'. Others contrast IBE with inductive inference, as we have done above. On this way of cutting the pie, 'inductive inference' is reserved for inferences from examined to unexamined instances of a given kind, of the sort we examined earlier; IBE and inductive inference are then two different types of non-deductive inference. Nothing hangs on which choice of terminology we favour, so long as we stick to it consistently.

Scientists frequently use IBE. For example, Darwin argued for his theory of evolution by calling attention to various facts about the living world which are hard to explain if we assume that current species have been separately created, but which make perfect sense if current species have descended from common ancestors, as his theory held. For example, there are close anatomical similarities between the legs of horses and zebras. How do we explain this, if God created horses and zebras separately? Presumably he could have made their legs as different as he pleased. But if horses and zebras have both descended from a recent common ancestor, this provides an obvious explanation of their anatomical similarity. Darwin argued that the ability of his theory to explain facts of this sort, and of many other sorts too, constituted strong evidence for its truth.

Another example of IBE is Einstein's famous work on Brownian motion. Brownian motion refers to the chaotic, zig-zag motion of microscopic particles suspended in a liquid or gas. It was discovered in 1827 by the Scottish botanist Robert Brown (1713–1858), while examining pollen grains floating in water. A number of attempted explanations of Brownian motion were advanced in the 19th century. One theory attributed the motion to electrical attraction between particles, another to agitation from external surroundings, and another to convection currents in the fluid. The correct explanation is based on the kinetic theory of matter, which says that liquids and gases are made up of atoms or molecules in motion. The suspended particles collide with the surrounding molecules, causing the erratic, random movements that Brown first observed. This theory was first proposed in the late 19th century but was not widely accepted, not least because many scientists didn't believe that atoms and molecules were real physical entities. But in 1905, Einstein provided an ingenious mathematical treatment of

Brownian motion, making a number of precise, quantitative predictions which were later confirmed experimentally. After Einstein's work, the kinetic theory was quickly agreed to provide a far better explanation of Brownian motion than any of the alternatives, and scepticism about the existence of atoms and molecules rapidly subsided.

One interesting question is whether IBE or ordinary induction is a more fundamental pattern of inference. The philosopher Gilbert Harman has argued that IBE is more fundamental. According to this view, whenever we make an ordinary inductive inference such as 'all pieces of metal examined so far conduct electricity, therefore all pieces of metal conduct electricity' we are implicitly appealing to explanatory considerations. We assume that the correct explanation for why the pieces of metal in our sample conducted electricity, whatever it is, entails that all pieces of metal will conduct electricity; that is why we make the inductive inference. But if we believed, for example, that the explanation for why the pieces of metal in our sample conducted electricity was that a laboratory technician had tinkered with them, we would not infer that all pieces of metal conduct electricity. Proponents of this view do not say there is no difference between IBE and ordinary induction – there clearly is. Rather, they think that ordinary induction is ultimately dependent on IBE.

However, other philosophers argue that this gets things backwards: IBE is itself parasitic on ordinary induction, they say. To see the grounds for this view, think back to the cheese-in-the-larder example above. Why do we regard the mouse hypothesis as a better explanation of the data than the maid hypothesis? Presumably, because we know that maids do not normally steal cheese, whereas mice do. But this is knowledge that we have gained through ordinary inductive reasoning, based on our previous observations of the behaviour of mice and maids. So according to this view, when we try to decide which of a group of competing hypotheses provides the best explanation of our data, we invariably appeal to knowledge that has been gained through ordinary induction. Thus it is incorrect to regard IBE as a more fundamental mode of inference.

Whichever of these opposing views we favour, one issue clearly demands more attention. If we want to use IBE, we need some way of deciding which of the competing hypotheses provides the best explanation of the data. But what criteria determine this? A popular answer is that the best explanation is the simplest or the most parsimonious one. Consider again the cheese-in-the-larder example. There are two pieces of data that need explaining: the missing cheese and the scratching noises. The mouse hypothesis postulates just one cause – a mouse – to explain both pieces of data. But the maid hypothesis must postulate two causes – a dishonest maid and an overheating boiler – to explain the same data. So the mouse hypothesis is more parsimonious, hence better. Similarly in the Darwin example, Darwin's theory could explain a very diverse range of facts about the living world, not just anatomical similarities between species. Each of these facts could be explained in other ways, as Darwin knew. But the theory of evolution explained all the facts in one go – that is what made it the best explanation of the data.

The idea that simplicity or parsimony is the mark of a good explanation is quite appealing, and certainly helps flesh out the idea of IBE. But if scientists use simplicity as a guide to inference, this raises a problem. For how do we know that the universe is simple rather than complex? Preferring a theory that explains the data in terms of the fewest number of causes does seem sensible. But is there any objective reason for thinking that such a theory is more likely to be true than a less simple theory? Philosophers of science do not agree on the answer to this difficult question.

Probability and induction

The concept of probability is philosophically puzzling. Part of the puzzle is that the word 'probability' seems to have more than one meaning. If you read that the probability of an Englishwoman living to 100 years of age is 1 in 10, you would understand this as saying that one-tenth of all Englishwomen live to the age of 100. Similarly, if you read that the probability of a male smoker developing lung cancer is 1 in 4, you would take this to mean that a quarter of all male smokers develop lung cancer. This is known as the frequency interpretation of probability: it equates probabilities with proportions, or frequencies. But what if you read that the probability of finding life on Mars is 1 in 1,000? Does this mean that one out of every thousand planets in our solar system contains life? Clearly it does not. For one thing, there are only nine planets in our solar system. So a different notion of probability must be at work here.

One interpretation of the statement 'the probability of life on Mars is 1 in 1,000' is that the person who utters it is simply reporting a subjective fact about themselves – they are telling us how likely they think life on Mars is. This is the subjective interpretation of probability. It takes probability to be a measure of the strength of our personal opinions. Clearly, we hold some of our opinions more strongly than others. I am very confident that Brazil will win the World Cup, reasonably confident that Jesus Christ existed, and rather less confident that global environmental disaster can be averted. This could be expressed by saying that I assign a high probability to the statement 'Brazil will win the World Cup', a fairly high probability to 'Jesus Christ existed', and a low probability to 'global environmental disaster can be averted'. Of course, to put an exact number on the strength of my conviction in these statements would be hard, but advocates of the subjective interpretation regard this as a merely practical limitation. In principle, we should be able to assign a precise numerical probability to each of the statements about which we have an opinion, reflecting how strongly we believe or disbelieve them, they say.

The subjective interpretation of probability implies that there are no objective facts about probability, independently of what people believe. If I say that the probability of finding life on Mars is high and you say that it is very low, neither of us is right or wrong – we are both simply stating how strongly we believe the statement in question. Of course, there is an objective fact about whether there is life on Mars or not; there is just no objective fact about how probable it is that there is life on Mars, according to the subjective interpretation.

The logical interpretation of probability rejects this position. It holds that a statement such as 'the probability of life on Mars is high' is objectively true or false, relative to a specified body of evidence. A statement's probability is the measure of the strength of evidence in its favour, on this view. Advocates of the logical interpretation think that for any two statements in our language, we can in principle discover the probability of one, given the other as evidence. For example, we might want to discover the probability that there will be an ice age within 10,000 years, given the current rate of global warming. The subjective interpretation says there is no objective fact about this probability. But the logical interpretation insists that there is: the current rate of global warming confers a definite numerical probability on the occurrence of an ice age within 10,000 years, say 0.9 for example. A probability of 0.9 clearly counts as a high probability – for the maximum is 1 – so the statement 'the probability that there will be an ice age within 10,000 years is high' would then be objectively true, given the evidence about global warming.

If you have studied probability or statistics, you may be puzzled by this talk of different interpretations of probability. How do these interpretations tie in with what you learned? The answer is that the mathematical study of probability does not by itself tell us what probability means, which is what we have been examining above. Most statisticians would in fact favour the frequency interpretation, but the problem of how to interpret probability, like most philosophical problems, cannot be resolved mathematically. The mathematical formulae for working out probabilities remain the same, whichever interpretation we adopt.

Philosophers of science are interested in probability for two main reasons. The first is that in many branches of science, especially physics and biology, we find laws and theories that are formulated using the notion of probability. Consider, for example, the theory known as Mendelian genetics, which deals with the transmission of genes from one generation to another in sexually reproducing populations. One of the most important principles of Mendelian genetics is that every gene in an organism has a 50% chance of making it into any one of the organism's gametes (sperm or egg cells). Hence there is a 50% chance that any gene found in your mother will also be in you, and likewise for the genes in your father. Using this principle and others, geneticists can provide detailed explanations for why particular characteristics (e.g. eye colour) are distributed across the generations of a family in the way that they are. Now 'chance' is just another word for probability, so it is obvious that our Mendelian principle makes essential use of the concept of probability. Many other examples could be given of scientific laws and principles that are expressed in terms of probability. The need to understand these laws and principles is an important motivation for the philosophical study of probability.

The second reason why philosophers of science are interested in the concept of probability is the hope that it might shed some light on inductive inference, in particular on Hume's problem; this shall be our focus here. At the root of Hume's problem is the fact that the premises of an inductive inference do not guarantee the truth of its conclusion. But it is tempting to suggest that the premises of a typical inductive inference do make the conclusion highly probable. Although the fact that all objects examined so far obey Newton's law of gravity doesn't prove that all objects do, surely it does make it very probable? So surely Hume's problem can be answered quite easily after all?

However, matters are not quite so simple. For we must ask what interpretation of probability this response to Hume assumes. On the frequency interpretation, to say it is highly probable that all objects obey Newton's law is to say that a very high proportion of all objects obey the law. But there is no way we can know that, unless we use induction! For we have only examined a tiny fraction of all the objects in the universe. So Hume's problem remains. Another way to see the point is this. We began with the inference from 'all examined objects obey Newton's law' to 'all objects obey Newton's law'. In response to Hume's worry that the premiss of this inference doesn't guarantee the truth of the conclusion, we suggested that it might nonetheless make the conclusion highly probable. But the inference from 'all examined objects obey Newton's law' to 'it is highly probable that all objects obey Newton's law' is still an inductive inference, given that the latter means 'a very high proportion of all objects obey Newton's law', as it does according to the frequency interpretation. So appealing to the concept of probability does not take the sting out of Hume's argument, if we adopt a frequency interpretation of probability. For knowledge of probabilities then becomes itself dependent on induction.

The subjective interpretation of probability is also powerless to solve Hume's problem, though for a different reason. Suppose John believes that the sun will rise tomorrow and Jack believes it will not. They both accept the evidence that the sun has risen every day in the past. Intuitively, we want to say that John is rational and Jack isn't, because the evidence makes John's belief more probable. But if probability is simply a matter of subjective opinion, we cannot say this. All we can say is that John assigns a high probability to 'the sun will rise tomorrow' and Jack does not. If there are no objective facts about probability, then we cannot say that the conclusions of inductive inferences are objectively probable. So we have no explanation of why someone like Jack, who declines to use induction, is irrational. But Hume's problem is precisely the demand for such an explanation.

The logical interpretation of probability holds more promise of a satisfactory response to Hume. Suppose there is an objective fact about the probability that the sun will rise tomorrow, given that it has risen every day in the past. Suppose this probability is very high. Then we have an explanation of why John is rational and Jack isn't. For John and Jack both accept the evidence that the sun has risen every day in the past, but Jack fails to realize that this evidence makes it highly probable that the sun will rise tomorrow, while John does realize this. Regarding a statement's probability as a measure of the evidence in its favour, as the logical interpretation recommends, tallies neatly with our intuitive feeling that the premises of an inductive inference can make the conclusion highly probable, even if they cannot guarantee its truth.

Unsurprisingly, therefore, those philosophers who have tried to solve Hume's problem via the concept of probability have tended to favour the logical interpretation. (One of these was the famous economist John Maynard Keynes, whose early interests were in logic and philosophy.) Unfortunately, most people today believe that the logical interpretation of probability faces very serious, probably insuperable, difficulties. This is because all the attempts to work out the logical interpretation of probability in any detail have run up against a host of problems, both mathematical and philosophical. As a result, many philosophers today are inclined to reject outright the underlying assumption of the logical interpretation – that there are objective facts about the probability of one statement, given another. Rejecting this assumption leads naturally to the subjective interpretation of probability, but that, as we have seen, offers scant hope of a satisfactory response to Hume.

Even if Hume's problem is ultimately insoluble, as seems likely, thinking about the problem is still a valuable exercise. For reflecting on the problem of induction leads us into a thicket of interesting questions about the structure of scientific reasoning, the nature of rationality, the appropriate degree of confidence to place in science, the interpretation of probability, and more. Like most philosophical questions, these questions probably do not admit of final answers, but in grappling with them we learn much about the nature and limits of scientific knowledge.

Chapter 3
Explanation in science

One of the most important aims of science is to try and explain what happens in the world around us. Sometimes we seek explanations for practical ends. For example, we might want to know why the ozone layer is being depleted so quickly, in order to try and do something about it. In other cases we seek scientific explanations simply to satisfy our intellectual curiosity – we want to understand more about how the world works. Historically, the pursuit of scientific explanation has been motivated by both goals.

Quite often, modern science is successful in its aim of supplying explanations. For example, chemists can explain why sodium turns yellow when it burns. Astronomers can explain why solar eclipses occur when they do. Economists can explain why the yen declined in value in the 1980s. Geneticists can explain why male baldness tends to run in families. Neurophysiologists can explain why extreme oxygen deprivation leads to brain damage. You can probably think of many other examples of successful scientific explanations.

But what exactly *is* scientific explanation? What exactly does it mean to say that a phenomenon can be 'explained' by science? This is a question that has exercised philosophers since Aristotle, but our starting point will be a famous account of scientific explanation put forward in the 1950s by the American philosopher Carl Hempel.

Hempel's account is known as the *covering law* model of explanation, for reasons that will become clear.

Hempel's covering law model of explanation

The basic idea behind the covering law model is straightforward. Hempel noted that scientific explanations are usually given in response to what he called 'explanation-seeking why questions'. These are questions such as 'why is the earth not perfectly spherical?', 'why do women live longer than men?', and the like – they are demands for explanation. To give a scientific explanation is thus to provide a satisfactory answer to an explanation-seeking why question. If we could determine the essential features that such an answer must have, we would know what scientific explanation is.

Hempel suggested that scientific explanations typically have the logical structure of an argument, i.e. a set of premises followed by a conclusion. The conclusion states that the phenomenon that needs explaining actually occurs, and the premises tell us why the conclusion is true. Thus suppose someone asks why sugar dissolves in water. This is an explanation-seeking why question. To answer it, says Hempel, we must construct an argument whose conclusion is 'sugar dissolves in water' and whose premises tell us why this conclusion is true. The task of providing an account of scientific explanation then becomes the task of characterizing precisely the relation that must hold between a set of premises and a conclusion, in order for the former to count as an explanation of the latter. That was the problem Hempel set himself.

Hempel's answer to the problem was three-fold. Firstly, the premises should entail the conclusion, i.e. the argument should be a deductive one. Secondly, the premises should all be true. Thirdly, the premises should consist of at least one general law. General laws are things such as 'all metals conduct electricity', 'a body's acceleration varies inversely with its mass', 'all plants contain chlorophyll', and so on; they contrast with particular facts such as 'this piece of metal conducts electricity', 'the plant on my desk contains chlorophyll' and so on. General laws are sometimes called 'laws of nature'. Hempel allowed that a scientific explanation could appeal to particular facts as well as general laws, but he held that at least one general law was always essential. So to explain a phenomenon, on Hempel's conception, is to show that its occurrence follows deductively from a general law, perhaps supplemented by other laws and/or particular facts, all of which must be true.

To illustrate, suppose I am trying to explain why the plant on my desk has died. I might offer the following explanation. Owing to the poor light in my study, no sunlight has been reaching the plant; but sunlight is necessary for a plant to photosynthesize; and without photosynthesis a plant cannot make the carbohydrates it needs to survive, and so will die; therefore my plant died. This explanation fits Hempel's model exactly. It explains the death of the plant by deducing it from two true laws – that sunlight is necessary for photosynthesis, and that photosynthesis is necessary for survival – and one particular fact – that the plant was not getting any sunlight. Given the truth of the two laws and the particular fact, the death of the plant *had* to occur; that is why the former constitute a good explanation of the latter.

Schematically, Hempel's model of explanation can be written as follows:

General laws
Particular facts
⇒
Phenomenon to be explained

The phenomenon to be explained is called the *explanandum*, and the general laws and particular facts that do the explaining are called the *explanans*. The explanandum itself may be either a particular fact or a general law. In the example above, it was a particular fact – the death of my plant. But sometimes the things we want to explain are general. For example, we might wish to explain why exposure to the sun leads to skin cancer. This is a general law, not a particular fact. To explain it, we would need to deduce it from still more fundamental laws – presumably, laws about the impact of radiation on skin cells, combined with particular facts about the amount of radiation in sunlight. So the structure of a scientific explanation is essentially the same, whether the *explanandum*, i.e. the thing we are trying to explain, is particular or general.

It is easy to see why Hempel's model is called the covering law model of explanation. For according to the model, the essence of explanation is to show that the phenomenon to be explained is 'covered' by some general law of nature. There is certainly something appealing about this idea. For showing that a phenomenon is a consequence of a general law does in a sense take the mystery out of it – it renders it more intelligible. And in fact, scientific explanations do often fit the pattern Hempel describes. For example, Newton explained why the planets move in ellipses around the sun by showing that this can be deduced from his law of universal gravitation, along with some minor additional assumptions. Newton's explanation fits Hempel's model exactly: a phenomenon is explained by showing that it had to be so, given the laws of nature plus some additional facts. After Newton, there was no longer any mystery about why planetary orbits are elliptical.

Hempel was aware that not all scientific explanations fit his model exactly. For example, if you ask someone why Athens is always immersed in smog, they will probably say 'because of car exhaust pollution'. This is a perfectly acceptable scientific explanation, though it involves no mention of any laws. But Hempel would say that if the explanation were spelled out in full detail, laws would enter the picture. Presumably there is a law that says something like 'if carbon monoxide is released into the earth's atmosphere in sufficient concentration, smog clouds will form'. The full explanation of why Athens is bathed in smog would cite this law, along with the fact that car exhaust contains carbon monoxide and

Athens has lots of cars. In practice, we wouldn't spell out the explanation in this much detail unless we were being very pedantic. But if we were to spell it out, it would correspond quite well to the covering law pattern.

Hempel drew an interesting philosophical consequence from his model about the relation between explanation and prediction. He argued that these are two sides of the same coin. Whenever we give a covering law explanation of a phenomenon, the laws and particular facts we cite would have enabled us to predict the occurrence of the phenomenon, if we hadn't already known about it. To illustrate, consider again Newton's explanation of why planetary orbits are elliptical. This fact was known long before Newton explained it using his theory of gravity – it was discovered by Kepler. But if it had not been known, Newton would have been able to predict it from his theory of gravity, for his theory entails that planetary orbits are elliptical, given minor additional assumptions. Hempel expressed this by saying that every scientific explanation is potentially a prediction – it would have served to predict the phenomenon in question, had it not already been known. The converse was also true, Hempel thought: every reliable prediction is potentially an explanation. To illustrate, suppose scientists predict that mountain gorillas will be extinct by 2010, based on information about the destruction of their habitat. Suppose they turn out to be right. According to Hempel, the information they used to predict the gorillas' extinction before it happened will serve to explain that same fact after it has happened. Explanation and prediction are structurally symmetric.

Though the covering law model captures the structure of many actual scientific explanations quite well, it also faces a number of awkward counter-examples. These counter-examples fall into two classes. On the one hand, there are cases of genuine scientific explanations that do not fit the covering law model, even approximately. These cases suggest that Hempel's model is too strict – it excludes some *bona fide* scientific explanations. On the other hand, there are cases of things that *do* fit the covering law model, but intuitively do not count as genuine scientific explanations. These cases suggest that Hempel's model is too liberal – it allows in things that should be excluded. We will focus on counter-examples of the second sort.

The problem of symmetry

Suppose you are lying on the beach on a sunny day, and you notice that a flagpole is casting a shadow of 20 metres across the sand (Figure 8).

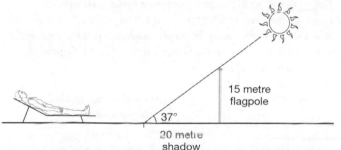

8. **A 15-metre flagpole casts a shadow of 20 metres on the beach when the sun is 37° overhead.**

Someone asks you to explain why the shadow is 20 metres long. This is an explanation-seeking why question. A plausible answer might go as follows: 'light rays from the sun are hitting the flagpole, which is exactly 15 metres high. The angle of elevation of the sun is 37°. Since light travels in straight lines, a simple trigonometric calculation (tan 37° = 15/20) shows that the flagpole will cast a shadow 20 metres long'.

This looks like a perfectly good scientific explanation. And by rewriting it in accordance with Hempel's schema, we can see that it fits the covering law model:

General laws	Light travels in straight lines
	Laws of trigonometry
Particular facts	Angle of elevation of the sun is 37°
	Flagpole is 15 metres high
⇒	
Phenomenon to be explained	Shadow is 20 metres long

The length of the shadow is deduced from the height of the flagpole and the angle of elevation of the sun, along with the optical law that light travels in straight lines and the laws of trigonometry. Since these laws are true, and since the flagpole is indeed 15 metres high, the explanation satisfies Hempel's requirements precisely. So far so good. The problem arises as follows. Suppose we swap the *explanandum* – that the shadow is 20 metres long – with the particular fact that the flagpole is 15 metres high. The result is this:

General law	Light travels in straight lines
	Laws of trigonometry
Particular facts	Angle of elevation of the sun is 37°
	Shadow is 20 metres long
⇒	
Phenomenon to be explained	Flagpole is 15 metres high

This 'explanation' clearly conforms to the covering law pattern too. The height of the flagpole is deduced from the length of the shadow it casts and the angle of elevation of the sun, along with the optical law that light travels in straight lines and the laws of trigonometry. But it seems very odd to regard this as an *explanation* of why the flagpole is 15 metres high. The real explanation of why the flagpole is 15 metres high is presumably that a carpenter deliberately made it so – it has nothing to do with the length of the shadow that it casts. So Hempel's model is too liberal: it allows something to count as a scientific explanation that obviously is not.

The general moral of the flagpole example is that the concept of explanation exhibits an important asymmetry. The height of the flagpole explains the length of the shadow, given the relevant laws and additional facts, but not vice-versa. In general, if x explains y, given the relevant laws and additional facts, then it will not be true that y explains x, given the same laws and facts. This is sometimes expressed by saying that explanation is an asymmetric relation. Hempel's covering law model does not respect this asymmetry. For just as we can deduce the length of the shadow from the height of the flagpole, given the laws and additional facts, so we can deduce the height of the flagpole from the length of the shadow. In other words, the covering law model implies that explanation should be a symmetric relation, but in fact it is asymmetric. So Hempel's model fails to capture fully what it is to be a scientific explanation.

The shadow and flagpole case also provides a counter-example to Hempel's thesis that explanation and prediction are two sides of the same coin. The reason is obvious. Suppose you didn't know how high the flagpole was. If someone told you that it was casting a shadow of 20 metres and that the sun was 37° overhead, you would be able to *predict* the flagpole's height, given that you knew the relevant optical and trigonometrical laws. But as we have just seen, this information clearly doesn't *explain* why the flagpole has the height it does. So in this example prediction and explanation part ways. Information that serves to predict a fact before we know it does not serve to explain that same fact after we know it, which contradicts Hempel's thesis.

The problem of irrelevance

Suppose a young child is in a hospital in a room full of pregnant women. The child notices that one person in the room – who is a man called John – is not pregnant, and asks the doctor why not. The doctor replies: 'John has been taking birth-control pills regularly for the last few years. People who take birth-control pills regularly never become pregnant. Therefore, John has not become pregnant'.

Let us suppose for the sake of argument that what the doctor says is true – John is mentally ill and does indeed take birth-control pills, which he believes help him. Even so, the doctor's reply to the child is clearly not very helpful. The correct explanation of why John has not become pregnant, obviously, is that he is male and males cannot become pregnant.

However, the explanation the doctor has given the child fits the covering law model perfectly. The doctor deduces the phenomenon to be explained – that John is not pregnant – from the general law that people who take birth-control pills do not become pregnant and the particular fact that John has been taking birth-control pills. Since both the general law and the particular fact are true, and since they do indeed entail the *explanandum*, according to the covering law model the doctor has given a perfectly adequate explanation of why John is not pregnant. But of course he hasn't. Hence the covering law model is again too permissive: it allows things to count as scientific explanations that intuitively are not.

The general moral is that a good explanation of a phenomenon should contain information that is *relevant* to the phenomenon's occurrence. This is where the doctor's reply to the child goes wrong. Although what the doctor tells the child is perfectly true, the fact that John has been taking birth-control pills is irrelevant to his not being pregnant, because he wouldn't have been pregnant even if he hadn't been taking the pills. This is why the doctor's reply does not constitute a good answer to the child's question. Hempel's model does not respect this crucial feature of our concept of explanation.

Explanation and causality

Since the covering law model encounters so many problems, it is natural to look for an alternative way of understanding scientific explanation. Some philosophers believe that the key lies in the concept of causality. This is quite an attractive suggestion. For in many cases to explain a phenomenon is indeed to say what caused it. For example, if an accident investigator is trying to explain an aeroplane crash, he is obviously looking for the cause of the crash. Indeed, the questions 'why did the plane crash?' and 'what was the cause of the plane crash?' are practically synonymous. Similarly, if an ecologist is trying to explain why there is less biodiversity in the tropical rainforests than there used to be, he is clearly looking for the cause of the reduction in biodiversity. The link between the concepts of explanation and causality is quite intimate.

Impressed by this link, a number of philosophers have abandoned the covering law account of explanation in favour of causality-based accounts. The details vary, but the basic idea behind these accounts is that to explain a phenomenon is simply to say what caused it. In some cases, the difference between the covering law and causal accounts is not actually very great, for to deduce the occurrence of a phenomenon from a general law often just *is* to give its cause. For example, recall again Newton's explanation of why planetary orbits are elliptical. We saw that this explanation fits the covering law model – for Newton deduced the shape of the planetary orbits from his law of gravity, plus some additional facts. But Newton's explanation was also a causal one, since elliptical planetary orbits are caused by the gravitational attraction between planets and the sun.

However, the covering law and causal accounts are not fully equivalent – in some cases they diverge. Indeed, many philosophers favour a causal account of explanation precisely because they think it can avoid some of the problems facing the covering law model. Recall the flagpole problem. Why do our intuitions tell us that the height of the flagpole explains the length of the shadow, given the laws, but not vice-versa? Plausibly, because the height of the flagpole is the cause of the shadow being 20 metres long, but the shadow being 20 metres long is not the cause of the flagpole being 15 metres high. So unlike the covering law model, a causal account of explanation gives the 'right' answer in the flagpole case – it respects our intuition that we cannot explain the height of the flagpole by pointing to the length of the shadow it casts.

The general moral of the flagpole problem was that the covering law model cannot accommodate the fact that explanation is an asymmetric relation. Now causality is obviously an asymmetric relation too: if x is the cause of y, then y is not the cause of x. For example, if the short-circuit caused the fire, then the fire clearly did not cause the short-circuit. It is therefore quite plausible to suggest that the asymmetry of explanation derives from the asymmetry of causality. If to explain a phenomenon is to say what caused it, then since causality is asymmetric we should expect explanation to be asymmetric too – as it is. The covering law model runs up against the flagpole problem precisely because it tries to analyse the concept of scientific explanation without reference to causality.

The same is true of the birth-control pill case. That John takes birth-control pills does not explain why he isn't pregnant, because the birth-control pills are not the cause of his not being pregnant. Rather, John's gender is the cause of his not being pregnant. That is why we think that the correct answer to the question 'why is John not pregnant?' is 'because he is a man, and men can't become pregnant', rather than the doctor's answer. The doctor's answer satisfies the covering law model, but since it does not correctly identify the cause of the phenomenon we wish to explain, it does not constitute a genuine explanation. The general moral we drew from the birth-control pill example was that a genuine scientific explanation must contain information that is relevant to the *explanandum*. In effect, this is another way of saying that the explanation should tell us the *explanandum*'s cause. Causality-based accounts of scientific explanation do not run up against the problem of irrelevance.

It is easy to criticize Hempel for failing to respect the close link between causality and explanation, and many people have done so.

In some ways, this criticism is a bit unfair. For Hempel subscribed to a philosophical doctrine known as *empiricism*, and empiricists are traditionally very suspicious of the concept of causality. Empiricism says that all our knowledge comes from experience. David Hume, whom we met in the last chapter, was a leading empiricist, and he argued that it is impossible to experience causal relations. So he concluded that they don't exist – causality is a figment of our imagination! This is a very hard conclusion to accept. Surely it is an objective fact that dropping glass vases causes them to break? Hume denied this. He allowed that it is an objective fact that most glass vases that have been dropped have in fact broken. But our idea of causality includes more than this. It includes the idea of a causal link between the dropping and the breaking, i.e. that the former brings about the latter. No such links are to be found in the world, according to Hume: all we see is a vase being dropped, and then it breaking a moment later. We experience no causal connection between the first event and the second. Causality is therefore a fiction.

Most empiricists have not accepted this startling conclusion outright. But as a result of Hume's work, they have tended to regard causality as a concept to be treated with great caution. So to an empiricist, the idea of analysing the concept of explanation in terms of the concept of causality would seem perverse. If one's goal is to clarify the concept of scientific explanation, as Hempel's was, there is little point in using notions that are equally in need of clarification themselves. And for empiricists, causality is definitely in need of philosophical clarification. So the fact that the covering law model makes no mention of causality was not a mere oversight on Hempel's part. In recent years, empiricism has declined somewhat in popularity. Furthermore, many philosophers have come to the conclusion that the concept of causality, although philosophically problematic, is indispensable to how we understand the world. So the idea of a causality-based account of scientific explanation seems more acceptable than it would have done in Hempel's day.

Causality-based accounts of explanation certainly capture the structure of many actual scientific explanations quite well, but are they the whole story? Many philosophers say no, on the grounds that certain scientific explanations do not seem to be causal. One type of example stems from what are called 'theoretical identifications' in science. Theoretical identifications involve identifying one concept with another, usually drawn from a different branch of science. 'Water is H_2O' is an example, as is 'temperature is average molecular kinetic energy'. In both of these cases, a familiar everyday concept is equated or identified with a more esoteric scientific concept. Often, theoretical identifications furnish us with what seem to be scientific explanations. When chemists discovered that water is H_2O, they thereby explained what water is. Similarly, when physicists discovered that an object's temperature is the average kinetic energy of its molecules, they thereby explained what temperature is. But neither of these explanations is causal. Being made of H_2O doesn't *cause* a substance to be water – it just *is* being water. Having a particular average molecular kinetic energy doesn't *cause* a liquid to have the temperature it does – it just *is* having that temperature. If these examples are accepted as legitimate scientific explanations, they suggest that causality-based accounts of explanation cannot be the whole story.

Can science explain everything?

Modern science can explain a great deal about the world we live in. But there are also numerous facts that have not been explained by science, or at least not explained fully. The origin of life is one such example. We know that about 4 billion years ago, molecules with the ability to make copies of themselves appeared in the primeval soup, and life evolved from there. But we do not understand how these self-replicating molecules got there in the first place. Another example is the fact that autistic children tend to have very good memories. Numerous studies of autistic children have confirmed this fact, but as yet nobody has succeeded in explaining it.

Many people believe that in the end, science will be able to explain facts of this sort. This is quite a plausible view. Molecular biologists are working hard on the problem of the origin of life, and only a pessimist would say they will never solve it. Admittedly, the problem is not easy, not least because it is very hard to know what conditions on earth 4 billion years ago were like. But nonetheless, there is no reason to think that the origin of life will never be explained. Similarly for the exceptional memories of autistic children. The science of memory is still in its infancy, and much remains to be discovered about the neurological basis of autism. Obviously we cannot guarantee that the explanation will eventually be found. But given the number of explanatory successes that modern science has already notched up, the smart money must be on many of today's unexplained facts eventually being explained too.

But does this mean that science can in principle explain everything? Or are there some phenomena that must forever elude scientific explanation? This is not an easy question to answer. On the one hand, it seems arrogant to assert that science can explain everything. On the other hand, it seems short-sighted to assert that any particular phenomenon can never be explained scientifically. For science changes and develops very fast, and a phenomenon that looks completely inexplicable from the vantage-point of today's science may be easily explained tomorrow.

According to some philosophers, there is a purely logical reason why science will never be able to explain everything. For in order to explain something, whatever it is, we need to invoke something else. But what explains the second thing? To illustrate, recall that Newton explained a diverse range of phenomena using his law of gravity. But what explains the law of gravity itself? If someone asks *why* all bodies exert a gravitational force on each other, what should we tell them? Newton had no answer to this question. In Newtonian science the law of gravity was a fundamental principle: it explained other things, but could not itself be explained. The moral is generalizable. However much the science of the future can explain, the explanations it gives will have to make use of certain fundamental laws and principles. Since nothing can explain itself, it follows that at least some of these laws and principles will themselves remain unexplained.

Whatever one makes of this argument, it is undeniably very abstract. It purports to show that some things will never be explained, but does not tell us what they are. However, some philosophers have made concrete suggestions about phenomena that they think science can never explain. An example is consciousness – the distinguishing feature of thinking, feeling creatures such as ourselves and other higher animals. Much research into the nature of consciousness has been and continues to be done, by brain scientists, psychologists, and others. But a number of recent philosophers claim that whatever this research throws up, it will never fully explain the nature of consciousness. There is something intrinsically mysterious about the phenomenon of consciousness, they maintain, that no amount of scientific investigation can eliminate.

What are the grounds for this view? The basic argument is that conscious experiences are fundamentally unlike anything else in the world, in that they have a 'subjective aspect'. Consider, for example, the experience of watching a terrifying horror movie. This is an experience with a very distinctive 'feel' to it; in the current jargon, there is 'something that it is like' to have the experience. Neuroscientists may one day be able to give a detailed account of the complex goings-on in the brain that produce our feeling of terror. But will this explain why watching a horror movie feels the way it does, rather than feeling some other way? Many people believe that it will not. On this view, the scientific study of the brain can at most tell us which brain processes are correlated with which conscious experiences. This is certainly interesting and valuable information. However, it doesn't tell us *why* experiences with distinctive subjective 'feels' should result from the purely physical goings-on in the brain. Hence consciousness, or at least one important aspect of it, is scientifically inexplicable.

Though quite compelling, this argument is very controversial and not endorsed by all philosophers, let alone all neuroscientists. Indeed, a well-known book published in 1991 by the philosopher Daniel Dennett is defiantly entitled *Consciousness Explained*. Supporters of the view that consciousness is scientifically inexplicable are sometimes accused of having a lack of imagination. Even if it is true that brain science as currently practised cannot explain the subjective aspect of conscious experience, can we not imagine the emergence of a radically different type of brain science, with radically different explanatory techniques, that *does* explain why our experiences feel the way they do? There is a long tradition of philosophers trying to tell scientists what is and isn't possible, and later scientific developments have often proved the philosophers wrong. Only time will tell whether the same fate awaits those who argue that consciousness must always elude scientific explanation.

Explanation and reduction

The different scientific disciplines are designed for explaining different types of phenomena. To explain why rubber doesn't conduct electricity is a task for physics. To explain why turtles have such long lives is a task for biology. To explain why higher interest rates reduce inflation is a task for economics, and so on. In short, there is a division of labour between the different sciences: each specializes in explaining its own particular set of phenomena. This explains why the sciences are not usually in competition with one another – why biologists, for example, do not worry that physicists and economists might encroach on their turf.

Nonetheless, it is widely held that the different branches of science are not all on a par: some are more fundamental than others. Physics is usually regarded as the most fundamental science of all.

Why? Because the objects studied by the other sciences are ultimately composed of physical particles. Consider living organisms, for example. Living organisms are made up of cells, which are themselves made up of water, nucleic acids (such as DNA), proteins, sugars, and lipids (fats), all of which consist of molecules or long chains of molecules joined together. But molecules are made up of atoms, which are physical particles. So the objects biologists study are ultimately just very complex physical entities. The same applies to the other sciences, even the social sciences. Take economics, for example. Economics studies the behaviour of corporations and consumers in the market place, and the consequences of this behaviour. But consumers are human beings and corporations are made up of human beings; and human beings are living organisms, hence physical entities.

Does this mean that, in principle, physics can subsume all the higher-level sciences? Since everything is made up of physical particles, surely if we had a complete physics, which allowed us to predict perfectly the behaviour of every physical particle in the universe, all the other sciences would become superfluous? Most philosophers resist this line of thought. After all, it seems crazy to suggest that physics might one day be able to explain the things that biology and economics explain. The prospect of deducing the laws of biology and economics straight from the laws of physics looks very remote. Whatever the physics of the future looks like, it is most unlikely to be capable of predicting economic downturns. Far from being reducible to physics, sciences such as biology and economics seem largely autonomous of it.

This leads to a philosophical puzzle. How can a science that studies entities that are ultimately physical *not* be reducible to physics? Granted that the higher-level sciences are in fact autonomous of physics, how is this possible? According to some philosophers, the answer lies in the fact that the objects studied by the higher-level sciences are 'multiply realized' at the physical level. To illustrate the idea of multiple realization, imagine a collection of ashtrays. Each individual ashtray is obviously a physical entity, like everything else in the universe. But the physical composition of the ashtrays could be very different – some might be made of glass, others of aluminium, others of plastic, and so on. And they will probably differ in size, shape, and weight. There is virtually no limit on the range of different physical properties that an ashtray can have. So it is impossible to define the concept 'ashtray' in purely physical terms. We cannot find a true statement of the form 'x is an ashtray if and only if x is . . . .' where the blank is filled by an expression taken from the language of physics. This means that ashtrays are multiply realized at the physical level.

Philosophers have often invoked multiple realization to explain why psychology cannot be reduced to physics or chemistry, but in principle the explanation works for any higher-level science. Consider, for example, the biological fact that nerve cells live longer than skin cells. Cells are physical entities, so one might think that this fact will one day be explained by physics. However, cells are almost certainly multiply realized at the microphysical level. Cells are ultimately made up of atoms, but the precise arrangement of atoms will be very different in different cells. So the concept 'cell' cannot be defined in terms drawn from fundamental physics. There is no true statement of the form 'x is a cell if and only if x is . . . ' where the blank is filled by an expression taken from the language of microphysics. If this is correct, it means that fundamental physics will never be able to explain why nerve cells live longer than skin cells, or indeed any other facts about cells. The vocabulary of cell biology and the vocabulary of physics do not map onto each other in the required way. Thus we have an explanation of why it is that cell biology cannot be reduced to physics, despite the fact that cells are physical entities. Not all philosophers are happy with the doctrine of multiple realization, but it does promise to provide a neat explanation of the autonomy of the higher-level sciences, both from physics and from each other.

Chapter 4
Realism and anti-realism

There is a very ancient debate in philosophy between two opposing schools of thought called *realism* and *idealism*. Realism holds that the physical world exists independently of human thought and perception. Idealism denies this – it claims that the physical world is in some way dependent on the conscious activity of humans. To most people, realism seems more plausible than idealism. For realism fits well with the common-sense view that the facts about the world are 'out there' waiting to be discovered by us, but idealism does not. Indeed, at first glance idealism can sound plain silly. Since rocks and trees would presumably continue to exist even if the human race died out, in what sense is their existence dependent on human minds? In fact, the issue is a bit more subtle than this, and continues to be discussed by philosophers today.

Though the traditional realism/idealism issue belongs to an area of philosophy called *metaphysics*, it has actually got nothing in particular to do with science. Our concern in this chapter is with a more modern debate that is specifically about science, and is in some ways analogous to the traditional issue. The debate is between a position known as *scientific realism* and its converse, known as *anti-realism* or *instrumentalism*. From now on, we shall use the word 'realism' to mean scientific realism, and 'realist' to mean scientific realist.

Scientific realism and anti-realism

Like most philosophical 'isms', scientific realism comes in many
different versions, so cannot be defined in a totally precise way. But
the basic idea is straightforward. Realists hold that the aim of
science is to provide a true description of the world. This may sound
like a fairly innocuous doctrine. For surely no-one thinks science is
aiming to produce a false description of the world. But that is not
what anti-realists think. Rather, anti-realists hold that the aim of
science is to provide a true description of a certain *part* of the
world – the 'observable' part. As far as the 'unobservable' part of
the world goes, it makes no odds whether what science says is true
or not, according to anti-realists.

What exactly do anti-realists mean by the observable part of the
world? They mean the everyday world of tables and chairs, trees
and animals, test-tubes and Bunsen burners, thunderstorms and
snow showers, and so on. Things such as these can be directly
perceived by human beings – that is what it means to call them
observable. Some branches of science deal exclusively with objects
that are observable. An example is palaeontology, or the study of
fossils. Fossils are readily observable – anyone with normally
functioning eyesight can see them. But other sciences make claims
about the unobservable region of reality. Physics is the obvious
example. Physicists advance theories about atoms, electrons,
quarks, leptons, and other strange particles, none of which can be
observed in the normal sense of the word. Entities of this sort lie
beyond the reach of the observational powers of humans.

With respect to sciences like palaeontology, realists and anti-realists
do not disagree. Since fossils are observable, the realist thesis that
science aims to truly describe the world and the anti-realist thesis
that science aims to truly describe the observable world obviously
coincide, as far as the study of fossils is concerned. But when it
comes to sciences like physics, realists and anti-realists disagree.
Realists say that when physicists put forward theories about

electrons and quarks, they are trying to provide a true description of the subatomic world, just as paleontologists are trying to provide a true description of the world of fossils. Anti-realists disagree: they see a fundamental difference between theories in subatomic physics and in palaeontology.

What do anti-realists think physicists *are* up to when they talk about unobservable entities? Typically they claim that these entities are merely convenient fictions, introduced by physicists in order to help predict observable phenomena. To illustrate, consider the kinetic theory of gases, which says that any volume of a gas contains a large number of very small entities in motion. These entities – molecules – are unobservable. From the kinetic theory we can deduce various consequences about the observable behaviour of gases, e.g. that heating a sample of gas will cause it to expand if the pressure remains constant, which can be verified experimentally. According to anti-realists, the only purpose of positing unobservable entities in the kinetic theory is to deduce consequences of this sort. Whether or not gases really *do* contain molecules in motion doesn't matter; the point of the kinetic theory is not to truly describe the hidden facts, but just to provide a convenient way of predicting observations. We can see why anti-realism is sometimes called 'instrumentalism' – it regards scientific theories as instruments for helping us predict observational phenomena, rather than as attempts to describe the underlying nature of reality.

Since the realism/anti-realism debate concerns the aim of science, one might think it could be resolved by simply asking the scientists themselves. Why not do a straw poll of scientists asking them about their aims? But this suggestion misses the point – it takes the expression 'the aim of science' too literally. When we ask what the aim of science is, we are not asking about the aims of individual scientists. Rather, we are asking how best to make sense of what scientists say and do – how to interpret the scientific enterprise. Realists think we should interpret all scientific theories as attempted descriptions of reality; anti-realists think this interpretation is inappropriate for theories that talk about unobservable entities and processes. While it would certainly be interesting to discover scientists' own views on the realism/anti-realism debate, the issue is ultimately a philosophical one.

Much of the motivation for anti-realism stems from the belief that we cannot actually attain knowledge of the unobservable part of reality – it lies beyond human ken. On this view, the limits to scientific knowledge are set by our powers of observation. So science can give us knowledge of fossils, trees, and sugar crystals, but not of atoms, electrons, and quarks – for the latter are unobservable. This view is not altogether implausible. For no-one could seriously doubt the existence of fossils and trees, but the same is not true of atoms and electrons. As we saw in the last chapter, in the late 19th century many leading scientists did doubt the existence of atoms. Anyone who accepts such a view must obviously give some explanation of *why* scientists advance theories about unobservable entities, if scientific knowledge is limited to what can be observed. The explanation anti-realists give is that they are convenient fictions, designed to help predict the behaviour of things in the observable world.

Realists do not agree that scientific knowledge is limited by our powers of observation. On the contrary, they believe we already have substantial knowledge of unobservable reality. For there is every reason to believe that our best scientific theories are true, and our best scientific theories talk about unobservable entities. Consider, for example, the atomic theory of matter, which says that all matter is made up of atoms. The atomic theory is capable of explaining a great range of facts about the world. According to realists, that is good evidence that the theory is true, i.e. that matter really is made up of atoms that behave as the theory says. Of course the theory *might* be false, despite the apparent evidence in its favour, but so might any theory. Just because atoms are unobservable, that is no reason to interpret atomic theory as anything other than an attempted description of reality – and a very successful one, in all likelihood.

Strictly we should distinguish two sorts of anti-realism. According to the first sort, talk of unobservable entities is not to be understood literally at all. So when a scientist puts forward a theory about electrons, for example, we should not take him to be asserting the existence of entities called 'electrons'. Rather, his talk of electrons is metaphorical. This form of anti-realism was popular in the first half of the 20th century, but few people advocate it today. It was motivated largely by a doctrine in the philosophy of language, according to which it is not possible to make meaningful assertions about things that cannot in principle be observed, a doctrine that few contemporary philosophers accept. The second sort of anti-realism accepts that talk of unobservable entities should be taken at face value: if a theory says that electrons are negatively charged, it is true if electrons do exist and are negatively charged, but false otherwise. But we will never know which, says the anti-realist. So the correct attitude towards the claims that scientists make about unobservable reality is one of total agnosticism. They are either true or false, but we are incapable of finding out which. Most modern anti-realism is of this second sort.

The 'no miracles' argument

Many theories that posit unobservable entities are *empirically successful* – they make excellent predictions about the behaviour of objects in the observable world. The kinetic theory of gases, mentioned above, is one example, and there are many others. Furthermore, such theories often have important technological applications. For example, laser technology is based on a theory about what happens when electrons in an atom go from higher to lower energy-states. And lasers work – they allow us to correct our vision, attack our enemies with guided missiles, and do much more besides. The theory that underpins laser technology is therefore highly empirically successful.

The empirical success of theories that posit unobservable entities is the basis of one of the strongest arguments for scientific realism, called the 'no miracles' argument. According to this argument, it would be an extraordinary coincidence if a theory that talks about electrons and atoms made accurate predictions about the observable world – unless electrons and atoms actually exist. If there are no atoms and electrons, what explains the theory's close fit with the observational data? Similarly, how do we explain the technological advances our theories have led to, unless by supposing that the theories in question are true? If atoms and electrons are just 'convenient fictions', as anti-realists maintain, then why do lasers work? On this view, being an anti-realist is akin to believing in miracles. Since it is obviously better not to believe in miracles if a non-miraculous alternative is available, we should be realists not anti-realists.

This argument is not intended to *prove* that realism is right and anti-realism wrong. Rather it is a plausibility argument – an inference to the best explanation. The phenomenon to be explained is the fact that many theories that postulate unobservable entities enjoy a high level of empirical success. The best explanation of this fact, say advocates of the 'no miracles' argument, is that the theories are true – the entities in question really exist, and behave just as the theories say. Unless we accept this explanation, the empirical success of our theories is an unexplained mystery.

Anti-realists have responded to the 'no miracles' argument in various ways. One response appeals to certain facts about the history of science. Historically, there are many cases of theories that we now believe to be false but that were empirically quite successful in their day. In a well-known article, the American philosopher of science Larry Laudan lists more than 30 such theories, drawn from a range of different scientific disciplines and eras. The phlogiston theory of combustion is one example. This theory, which was widely accepted until the end of the 18th century, held that when any object burns it releases a substance called 'phlogiston' into the atmosphere. Modern chemistry teaches us that this is false: there is no such substance as phlogiston. Rather, burning occurs when things react with oxygen in the air. But despite the non-existence of phlogiston, the phlogiston theory was empirically quite successful: it fitted the observational data available at the time reasonably well.

Examples of this sort suggest that the 'no miracles' argument for scientific realism is a bit too quick. Proponents of that argument regard the empirical success of today's scientific theories as evidence of their truth. But the history of science shows that empirically successful theories have often turned out to be false. So how do we know that the same fate will not befall today's theories? How do we know that the atomic theory of matter, for example, will not go the same way as the phlogiston theory? Once we pay due attention to the history of science, argue the anti-realists, we see that the inference from empirical success to theoretical truth is a very shaky one. The rational attitude towards the atomic theory is thus one of agnosticism – it may be true, or it may not. We just do not know, say the anti-realists.

This is a powerful counter to the 'no miracles' argument, but it is not completely decisive. Some realists have responded by modifying the argument slightly. According to the modified version, the empirical success of a theory is evidence that what the theory says about the unobservable world is approximately true, rather than precisely true. This weaker claim is less vulnerable to counter-examples from the history of science. It is also more modest: it allows the realist to admit that today's theories may not be correct down to every last detail, while still holding that they are broadly on the right lines. Another way of modifying the argument is by refining the notion of empirical success. Some realists hold that empirical success is not just a matter of fitting the known observational data, but rather allowing us to predict new observational phenomena that were previously unknown. Relative to this more stringent criterion of empirical success, it is less easy to find historical examples of empirically successful theories that later turned out to be false.

Whether these refinements can really save the 'no miracles' argument is debatable. They certainly reduce the number of historical counter-examples, but not to zero. One that remains is the wave theory of light, first put forward by Christian Huygens in 1690. According to this theory, light consists of wave-like vibrations in an invisible medium called the ether, which was supposed to permeate the whole universe. (The rival to the wave theory was the particle theory of light, favoured by Newton, which held that light consists of very small particles emitted by the light source.) The wave theory was not widely accepted until the French physicist Auguste Fresnel formulated a mathematical version of the theory in 1815, and used it to predict some surprising new optical phenomena. Optical experiments confirmed Fresnel's predictions, convincing many 19th-century scientists that the wave theory of light must be true. But modern physics tells us the theory is not true: there is no such thing as the ether, so light doesn't consist of vibrations in it. Again, we have an example of a false but empirically successful theory.

The important feature of this example is that it tells against even the modified version of the 'no miracles' argument. For Fresnel's theory *did* make novel predictions, so qualifies as empirically successful even relative to the stricter notion of empirical success. And it is hard to see how Fresnel's theory can be called 'approximately true', given that it was based around the idea of the ether, which does not exist. Whatever exactly it means for a theory to be approximately true, a necessary condition is surely that the entities the theory talks about really do exist. In short, Fresnel's theory was empirically successful even according to a strict understanding of this notion, but was not even approximately true. The moral of the story, say anti-realists, is that we should not assume that modern scientific theories are even roughly on the right lines, just because they are so empirically successful.

Whether the 'no miracles' argument is a good argument for scientific realism is therefore an open question. On the one hand, the argument is open to quite serious objections, as we have seen. On the other hand, there is something intuitively compelling about the argument. It really is hard to accept that atoms and electrons might not exist, when one considers the amazing success of theories that postulate these entities. But as the history of science shows, we should be very cautious about assuming that our current scientific theories are true, however well they fit the data. Many people have assumed that in the past and been proved wrong.

The observable/unobservable distinction

Central to the debate between realism and anti-realism is the distinction between things that are observable and things that are not. So far we have simply taken this distinction for granted – tables and chairs are observable, atoms and electrons are not. But in fact the distinction is quite philosophically problematic. Indeed, one of the main arguments for scientific realism says that it is not possible to draw the observable/unobservable distinction in a principled way.

Why should this be an argument for scientific realism? Because the coherence of anti-realism is crucially dependent on there being a clear distinction between the observable and the unobservable. Recall that anti-realists advocate a different attitude towards scientific claims, depending on whether they are about observable or unobservable parts of reality – we should remain agnostic about the truth of the latter, but not the former. Anti-realism thus presupposes that we can divide scientific claims into two sorts: those that are about observable entities and processes, and those that are not. If it turns out that this division cannot be made in a satisfactory way, then anti-realism is obviously in serious trouble, and realism wins by default. That is why scientific realists are often keen to emphasize the problems associated with the observable/unobservable distinction.

One such problem concerns the relation between observation and detection. Entities such as electrons are obviously not observable in the ordinary sense, but their presence can be detected using special pieces of apparatus called particle detectors. The simplest particle detector is the cloud chamber, which consists of a closed container filled with air that has been saturated with water-vapour (Figure 9). When charged particles such as electrons pass through the chamber, they collide with neutral atoms in the air, converting them into ions; water vapour condenses around these ions causing liquid droplets to form, which can be seen with the naked eye. We can follow the path of an electron through the cloud chamber by watching the tracks of these liquid droplets. Does this mean that electrons can be observed after all? Most philosophers would say no: cloud chambers allow us to detect electrons, not observe them directly. In much the same way, high-speed jets can be detected by the vapour trails they leave behind, but watching these trails is not observing the jet. But is it always clear how to distinguish observing from detecting? If not, then the anti-realist position could be in trouble.

In a well-known defence of scientific realism from the early 1960s, the American philosopher Grover Maxwell posed the following problem for the anti-realist. Consider the following sequence of events: looking at something with the naked eye, looking at something through a window, looking at something through a pair of strong glasses, looking at something through binoculars, looking at something though a low-powered microscope, looking at something through a high-powered microscope, and so on. Maxwell argued that these events lie on a smooth continuum. So how do we decide which count as observing and which not? Can a biologist observe micro-organisms with his high-powered microscope, or can he only detect their presence in the way that a physicist can detect the presence of electrons in a cloud chamber? If something can only be seen with the help of sophisticated scientific instruments, does it count as observable or unobservable? How sophisticated can the instrumentation be, before we have a case of detecting rather

9. One of the first photographs to show the tracks of subatomic particles in a cloud chamber. The picture was taken by the cloud chamber's inventor, English physicist C. T. R. Wilson, at the Cavendish Laboratory in Cambridge in 1911. The tracks are due to alpha particles emitted by a small amount of radium on the top of a metal tongue inserted into the cloud chamber. As an electrically charged particle moves through the water vapour in a cloud chamber, it ionizes the gas, and water drops condense on the ions, thus producing a track of droplets where the particle has passed.

than observing? There is no principled way of answering these questions, Maxwell argued, so the anti-realist's attempt to classify entities as either observable or unobservable is doomed to failure.

Maxwell's argument is bolstered by the fact that scientists themselves sometimes talk about 'observing' particles with the help of sophisticated bits of apparatus. In the philosophical literature, electrons are usually taken as paradigm examples of unobservable entities, but scientists are often perfectly happy to talk about 'observing' electrons using particle detectors. Of course, this does not prove that the philosophers are wrong and that electrons are observable after all, for the scientists' talk is probably best regarded as a *façon-de-parler*. Similarly, the fact that scientists talk about having 'experimental proof' of a theory does not mean that experiments can really prove theories to be true, as we saw in Chapter 2. Nonetheless, if there really is a philosophically important observable/unobservable distinction, as anti-realists maintain, it is odd that it corresponds so badly with the way scientists themselves speak.

Maxwell's arguments are powerful, but by no means completely decisive. Bas van Fraassen, a leading contemporary anti-realist, claims that Maxwell's arguments only show 'observable' to be a vague concept. A vague concept is one that has borderline cases – cases that neither clearly do nor clearly do not fall under it. 'Bald' is an obvious example. Since hair loss comes in degrees, there are many men of whom it's hard to say whether they are bald or not. But van Fraassen points out that vague concepts are perfectly usable, and can mark genuine distinctions in the world. (In fact, most concepts are vague to at least some extent.) No-one would argue that the distinction between bald and hirsute men is unreal or unimportant simply because 'bald' is vague. Certainly, if we attempt to draw a sharp dividing line between bald and hirsute men, it will arbitrary. But since there are clear-cut cases of men who are bald and clear-cut cases of men who are not, the impossibility of drawing a sharp dividing line doesn't matter. The concept is perfectly usable despite its vagueness.

Precisely the same applies to 'observable', according to van Fraassen. There are clear-cut cases of entities that can be observed, for example chairs, and clear-cut cases of entities that cannot, for example electrons. Maxwell's argument highlights the fact that there are also borderline cases, where we are unsure whether the entities in question can be observed or only detected. So if we try to draw a sharp dividing line between observable and unobservable entities, it will inevitably be somewhat arbitrary. But as with baldness, this does not show that the observable/unobservable distinction is somehow unreal or unimportant, for there are clear-cut cases on either side. So the vagueness of the term 'observable' is no embarrassment to the anti-realist, van Fraassen argues. It only sets an upper limit on the precision with which she can formulate her position.

How strong an argument is this? Van Fraassen is certainly right that the existence of borderline cases, and the consequent impossibility of drawing a sharp boundary without arbitrariness, does not show the observable/unobservable distinction to be unreal. To that extent, his argument against Maxwell succeeds. However, it is one thing to show that there is a real distinction between observable and unobservable entities, and another to show that the distinction is capable of bearing the philosophical weight that anti-realists wish to place on it. Recall that anti-realists advocate an attitude of complete agnosticism towards claims about the unobservable part of reality – we have no way of knowing whether they are true or not, they say. Even if we grant van Fraassen his point that there are clear cases of unobservable entities, and that that is enough for the anti-realist to be getting on with, the anti-realist still needs to provide an argument for thinking that knowledge of unobservable reality is impossible.

Philosophy of Science

70

The underdetermination argument

One argument for anti-realism centres on the relationship between scientists' observational data and their theoretical claims. Anti-realists emphasize that the ultimate data to which scientific theories are responsible is always observational in character. (Many realists would agree with this claim.) To illustrate, consider again the kinetic theory of gases, which says that any sample of gas consists of molecules in motion. Since these molecules are unobservable, we obviously cannot test the theory by directly observing various samples of gas. Rather, we need to deduce from the theory some statement that can be directly tested, which will invariably be about observable entities. As we saw, the kinetic theory implies that a sample of gas will expand when heated, if the pressure remains constant. This statement can be directly tested, by observing the readings on the relevant pieces of apparatus in a laboratory (Figure 10). This example illustrates a general truth: observational data

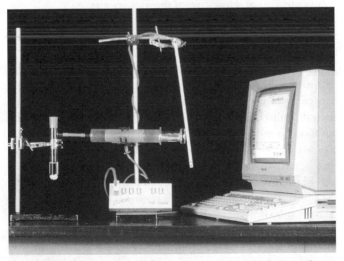

10. Dialatometer for measuring the change in volume of a gas as its temperature varies.

constitute the ultimate evidence for claims about unobservable entities.

Anti-realists then argue that the observational data 'underdetermine' the theories scientists put forward on their basis. What does this mean? It means that the data can in principle be explained by many different, mutually incompatible, theories. In the case of the kinetic theory, anti-realists will say that *one* possible explanation of the observational data is that gases contain large numbers of molecules in motion, as the kinetic theory says. But they will insist that there are other possible explanations too, which conflict with the kinetic theory. So according to anti-realists, scientific theories that posit unobservable entities are underdetermined by the observational data – there will always be a number of competing theories that can account for that data equally well.

It is easy to see why the underdetermination argument supports an anti-realist view of science. For if theories are always underdetermined by the observational data, how can we ever have reason to believe that a particular theory is true? Suppose a scientist advocates a given theory about unobservable entities, on the grounds that it can explain a large range of observational data. An anti-realist philosopher of science comes along, and argues that the data can in fact be accounted for by various alternative theories. If the anti-realist is correct, it follows that the scientist's confidence in her theory is misplaced. For what reason does the scientist have to choose the theory she does, rather than one of the alternatives? In such a situation, surely the scientist should admit that she has no idea which theory is true? Underdetermination leads naturally to the anti-realist conclusion that agnosticism is the correct attitude to take towards claims about the unobservable region of reality.

But is it actually true that a given set of observational data can always be explained by many different theories, as anti-realists maintain? Realists usually respond to the underdetermination argument by insisting that this claim is true only in a trivial and uninteresting sense. In principle, there will always be more than one possible explanation of a given set of observations. But, say the realists, it does not follow that all of these possible explanations are as good as one another. Just because two theories can both account for our observational data does not mean that there is nothing to choose between them. For one of the theories might be simpler than the other, for example, or might explain the data in a more intuitively plausible way, or might postulate fewer hidden causes, and so on. Once we acknowledge that there are criteria for theory choice in addition to compatibility with the observational data, the problem of underdetermination disappears. Not all the possible explanations of our observational data are as good as one another. Even if the data that the kinetic theory explains can in principle be explained by alternative theories, it does not follow that these alternatives can explain as well as the kinetic theory does.

This response to the underdetermination argument is bolstered by the fact that there are relatively few real cases of underdetermination in the history of science. If the observational data can always be explained equally well by many different theories, as anti-realists maintain, surely we should expect to find scientists in near perpetual disagreement with one another? But that is not what we find. Indeed, when we inspect the historical record, the situation is almost exactly the reverse of what the underdetermination argument would lead us to expect. Far from scientists being faced with a large number of alternative explanations of their observational data, they often have difficulty finding even *one* theory that fits the data adequately. This lends support to the realist view that underdetermination is merely a philosopher's worry, with little relation to actual scientific practice.

Anti-realists are unlikely to be impressed by this response. After all, philosophical worries are still genuine ones, even if their practical implications are few. Philosophy may not change the world, but that doesn't mean it isn't important. And the suggestion that criteria such as simplicity can be used to adjudicate between competing theories immediately invites the awkward question of why simpler theories should be thought more likely to be true; we touched on this issue in Chapter 2. Anti-realists typically grant that the problem of underdetermination can be eliminated in practice by using criteria such as simplicity to discriminate between competing explanations of our observational data. But they deny that such criteria are reliable indicators of the truth. Simpler theories may be more convenient to work with, but they are not intrinsically more probable than complex ones. So the underdetermination argument stands: there are always multiple explanations of our data, we have no way of knowing which is true, so knowledge of unobservable reality cannot be had.

However, the story does not end here; there is a further realist comeback. Realists accuse anti-realists of applying the underdetermination argument selectively. If the argument is applied consistently, it rules out not only knowledge of the unobservable world, but also knowledge of much of the observable world, say the realists. To understand why realists say this, notice that many things that are observable never actually get observed. For example, the vast majority of living organisms on the planet never get observed by humans, but they are clearly observable. Or think of an event such as a large meteorite hitting the earth. No-one has ever witnessed such an event, but it is clearly observable. It just so happens that no human was ever in the right place at the right time. Only a small fraction of what is observable actually gets observed.

The key point is this. Anti-realists claim that the unobservable part of reality lies beyond the limits of scientific knowledge. So they allow that we can have knowledge of objects and events that are observable but unobserv*ed*. But theories about unobserv*ed* objects and events are just as underdetermined by our data as are theories about unobserv*able* ones. For example, suppose a scientist puts forward the hypothesis that a meteorite struck the moon in 1987.

He cites various pieces of observational data to support this hypothesis, e.g. that satellite pictures of the moon show a large crater that wasn't there before 1987. However, this data can in principle be explained by many alternative hypotheses – perhaps a volcanic eruption caused the crater, or an earthquake. Or perhaps the camera that took the satellite pictures was faulty, and there is no crater at all. So the scientist's hypothesis is underdetermined by the data, even though the hypothesis is about a perfectly observable event – a meteorite striking the moon. If we apply the underdetermination argument consistently, say realists, we are forced to conclude that we can only acquire knowledge of things that have actually been observed.

This conclusion is very implausible, and is not one that any philosopher of science would wish to accept. For much of what scientists tell us concerns things that have not been observed – think of ice ages, dinosaurs, continental drift, and the like. To say that knowledge of the unobserved is impossible is to say that most of what passes for scientific knowledge is not really knowledge at all. Of course, scientific realists do not accept this conclusion. Rather, they take it as evidence that the underdetermination argument must be wrong. Since science clearly does give us knowledge of the unobserved, despite the fact that theories about the unobserved are underdetermined by our data, it follows that underdetermination is no barrier to knowledge. So the fact that our theories about the unobservable are also underdetermined by our data does not mean that science cannot give us knowledge of the unobservable region of the world.

In effect, realists who argue this way are saying that the problem raised by the underdetermination argument is simply a sophisticated version of the problem of induction. To say that a theory is underdetermined by the data is to say that there are alternative theories that can account for the same data. But this is effectively just to say that the data do not entail the theory: the inference from the data to the theory is non-deductive. Whether the theory is about unobservable entities, or about observable but unobserved entities, makes no difference – the logic of the situation is the same in both cases. Of course, showing that the underdetermination argument is just a version of the problem of induction does not mean that it can be ignored. For there is little consensus on how the problem of induction should be tackled, as we saw in Chapter 2. But it does mean that there is no *special* difficulty about unobservable entities. Therefore the anti-realist position is ultimately arbitrary, say the realists. Whatever problems there are in understanding how science can give us knowledge of atoms and electrons are equally problems for understanding how science can give us knowledge of ordinary, medium-sized objects.

Chapter 5
Scientific change and scientific revolutions

Scientific ideas change fast. Pick virtually any scientific discipline you like, and you can be sure that the prevalent theories in that discipline will be very different from those of 50 years ago, and extremely different from those of 100 years ago. Compared with other areas of intellectual endeavour such as philosophy and the arts, science is a rapidly changing activity. A number of interesting philosophical questions centre on the issue of scientific change. Is there a discernible pattern to the way scientific ideas change over time? When scientists abandon their existing theory in favour of a new one, how should we explain this? Are later scientific theories objectively better than earlier ones? Or does the concept of objectivity make sense at all?

Most modern discussion of these questions takes off from the work of the late Thomas Kuhn, an American historian and philosopher of science. In 1963 Kuhn published a book called *The Structure of Scientific Revolutions*, unquestionably the most influential work of philosophy of science in the last 50 years. The impact of Kuhn's ideas has also been felt in other academic disciplines such as sociology and anthropology, and in the general intellectual culture at large. (*The Guardian* newspaper included *The Structure of Scientific Revolutions* in its list of the 100 most influential books of the 20th century.) In order to understand why Kuhn's ideas caused such a stir, we need to look briefly at the state of philosophy of science prior to the publication of his book.

Logical positivist philosophy of science

The dominant philosophical movement in the English-speaking world in the post-war period was *logical positivism*. The original logical positivists were a loosely knit group of philosophers and scientists who met in Vienna in the 1920s and early 1930s, under the leadership of Moritz Schlick. (Carl Hempel, whom we met in Chapter 3, was closely associated with the positivists, as was Karl Popper.) Fleeing persecution by the Nazis, most of the positivists emigrated to the United States, where they and their followers exerted a powerful influence on academic philosophy until about the mid-1960s, by which time the movement had begun to disintegrate.

The logical positivists had a very high regard for the natural sciences, and also for mathematics and logic. The early years of the 20th century witnessed exciting scientific advances, particularly in physics, which impressed the positivists tremendously. One of their aims was to make philosophy itself more 'scientific', in the hope that this would allow similar advances to be made in philosophy. What particularly impressed the positivists about science was its apparent objectivity. Unlike in other fields, where much turned on the subjective opinion of enquirers, scientific questions could be settled in a fully objective way, they believed. Techniques such as experimental testing allowed a scientist to compare his theory directly with the facts, and thus reach an informed, unbiased decision about the theory's merits. Science for the positivists was thus a paradigmatically rational activity, the surest route to the truth that there is.

Despite the high esteem in which they held science, the positivists paid little attention to the history of science. Indeed, they believed that philosophers had little to learn from studying history of science. This was primarily because they drew a sharp distinction between what they called the 'context of discovery' and the 'context of justification'. The context of discovery refers to the actual historical process by which a scientist arrives at a given theory. The context of justification refers to the means by which the scientist tries to justify his theory once it is already there – which includes testing the theory, searching for relevant evidence, and so on. The positivists believed that the former was a subjective, psychological process that wasn't governed by precise rules, while the latter was an objective matter of logic. Philosophers of science should confine themselves to studying the latter, they argued.

An example can help make this idea clearer. In 1865 the Belgian scientist Kekule discovered that the benzene molecule has a hexagonal structure. Apparently, he hit on the hypothesis of a hexagonal structure for benzene after a dream in which he saw a snake trying to bite its own tail (Figure 11). Of course, Kekule then had to test his hypothesis scientifically, which he did. This is an extreme example, but it shows that scientific hypotheses can be arrived at in the most unlikely of ways – they are not always the product of careful, systematic thought. The positivists would argue that it makes no difference how a hypothesis is arrived at initially. What matters is how it is tested once it is already there – for it is this that makes science a rational activity. How Kekule first arrived at his hypothesis was immaterial; what mattered was how he justified it.

This sharp distinction between discovery and justification, and the belief that the former is 'subjective' and 'psychological' while the latter is not, explains why the positivists' approach to philosophy of science was so ahistorical. For the actual historical process by which scientific ideas change and develop lies squarely in the context of discovery, not the context of justification. That process might be of interest to historians or psychologists, but had nothing to teach philosophers of science, according to the positivists.

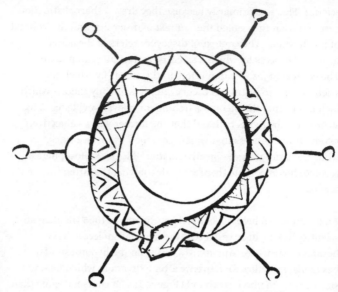

11. Kekule arrived at the hypothesis of the hexagonal structure of benzene after a dream in which he saw a snake trying to bite its own tail.

Another important theme in positivist philosophy of science was the distinction between theories and observational facts; this is related to the observable/unobservable distinction discussed in the previous chapter. The positivists believed that disputes between rival scientific theories could be solved in a perfectly objective way – by comparing the theories directly with the 'neutral' observational facts, which all parties could accept. The positivists disagreed between themselves about how exactly this set of neutral facts should be characterized, but they were adamant that it existed. Without a clear distinction between theories and observational facts, the rationality and objectivity of science would be compromised, and the positivists were resolute in their belief that science was rational and objective.

The structure of scientific revolutions

Kuhn was a historian of science by training, and firmly believed that philosophers had much to learn from studying the history of science. Insufficient attention to the history of science had led the positivists to form an inaccurate and naïve picture of the scientific enterprise, he maintained. As the title of his book indicates, Kuhn was especially interested in scientific revolutions – periods of great upheaval when existing scientific ideas are replaced with radically new ones. Examples of scientific revolutions are the Copernican revolution in astronomy, the Einsteinian revolution in physics, and the Darwinian revolution in biology. Each of these revolutions led to a fundamental change in the scientific world-view – the overthrow of an existing set of ideas by a completely different set.

Of course, scientific revolutions happen relatively infrequently – most of the time any given science is not in a state of revolution. Kuhn coined the term 'normal science' to describe the ordinary day-to-day activities that scientists engage in when their discipline is not undergoing revolutionary change. Central to Kuhn's account of normal science is the concept of a *paradigm*. A paradigm consists of two main components: firstly, a set of fundamental theoretical assumptions that all members of a scientific community accept at a given time; secondly, a set of 'exemplars' or particular scientific problems that have been solved by means of those theoretical assumptions, and that appear in the textbooks of the discipline in question. But a paradigm is more than just a theory (though Kuhn sometimes uses the words interchangeably). When scientists share a paradigm they do not just agree on certain scientific propositions, they agree also on how future scientific research in their field should proceed, on which problems are the pertinent ones to tackle, on what the appropriate methods for solving those problems are, on what an acceptable solution of the problems would look like, and so on. In short, a paradigm is an entire scientific outlook – a constellation of shared assumptions, beliefs, and values that unite a scientific community and allow normal science to take place.

What exactly does normal science involve? According to Kuhn it is primarily a matter of *puzzle-solving*. However successful a paradigm is, it will always encounter certain problems – phenomena that it cannot easily accommodate, mismatches between the theory's predictions and the experimental facts, and so on. The job of the normal scientist is to try to eliminate these minor puzzles while making as few changes as possible to the paradigm. So normal science is a highly conservative activity – its practitioners are not trying to make any earth-shattering discoveries, but rather just to develop and extend the existing paradigm. In Kuhn's words, 'normal science does not aim at novelties of fact or theory, and when successful finds none'. Above all, Kuhn stressed that normal scientists are not trying to *test* the paradigm. On the contrary, they accept the paradigm unquestioningly, and conduct their research within the limits it sets. If a normal scientist gets an experimental result that conflicts with the paradigm, she will usually assume that her experimental technique is faulty, not that the paradigm is wrong. The paradigm itself is not negotiable.

Typically, a period of normal science lasts many decades, sometimes even centuries. During this time scientists gradually articulate the paradigm – fine-tuning it, filling in details, solving more and more puzzles, extending its range of application, and so on. But over time *anomalies* are discovered – phenomena that simply cannot be reconciled with the theoretical assumptions of the paradigm, however hard normal scientists try. When anomalies are few in number they tend to just get ignored. But as more and more anomalies accumulate, a burgeoning sense of crisis envelops the scientific community. Confidence in the existing paradigm breaks down, and the process of normal science temporarily grinds to a halt. This marks the beginning of a period of 'revolutionary science' as Kuhn calls it. During such periods, fundamental scientific ideas *are* up for grabs. A variety of alternatives to the old paradigm are proposed, and eventually a new paradigm becomes established. A generation or so is usually required before all members of the scientific community are won over to the new paradigm – an event that marks the completion of a scientific revolution. The essence of a scientific revolution is thus the shift from an old paradigm to a new one.

Kuhn's characterization of the history of science as long periods of normal science punctuated by occasional scientific revolutions struck a chord with many philosophers and historians of science. A number of examples from the history of science fit Kuhn's model quite well. When we examine the transition from Ptolemaic to Copernican astronomy, for example, or from Newtonian to Einsteinian physics, many of the features that Kuhn describes are present. Ptolemaic astronomers did indeed share a paradigm, based around the theory that the earth is stationary at the centre of the universe, which formed the unquestioned back-drop to their investigations. The same is true of Newtonian physicists in the 18th and 19th centuries, whose paradigm was based around Newton's theory of mechanics and gravitation. And in both cases, Kuhn's account of how an old paradigm gets replaced by a new one applies fairly accurately. There are also scientific revolutions that do not fit the Kuhnian model so neatly – for example the recent molecular revolution in biology. But nonetheless, most people agree that Kuhn's description of the history of science contains much of value.

Why did Kuhn's ideas cause such a storm? Because in addition to his purely descriptive claims about the history of science, Kuhn advanced some highly controversial philosophical theses. Ordinarily we assume that when scientists trade their existing theory for a new one, they do so on the basis of objective evidence. But Kuhn argued that adopting a new paradigm involves a certain act of faith on the part of the scientist. He allowed that a scientist could have good reasons for abandoning an old paradigm for a new one, but he insisted that reasons alone could never rationally *compel* a paradigm shift. 'The transfer of allegiance from paradigm to paradigm', Kuhn wrote, 'is a conversion experience which cannot be forced'. And in explaining why a new paradigm rapidly gains acceptance in the scientific community, Kuhn emphasized the peer pressure of scientists on one another. If a given paradigm has very forceful advocates, it is more likely to win widespread acceptance.

Many of Kuhn's critics were appalled by these claims. For if paradigm shifts work the way Kuhn says, it is hard to see how science can be regarded as a rational activity at all. Surely scientists are meant to base their beliefs on evidence and reason, not on faith and peer pressure? Faced with two competing paradigms, surely the scientist should make an objective comparison of them to determine which has more evidence in its favour? Undergoing a 'conversion experience', or allowing oneself to be persuaded by the most forceful of one's fellow scientists, hardly seems like a rational way to behave. Kuhn's account of paradigm shifts seems hard to reconcile with the familiar positivist image of science as an objective, rational activity. One critic wrote that on Kuhn's account, theory choice in science was 'a matter for mob psychology'.

Kuhn also made some controversial claims about the overall direction of scientific change. According to a widely held view, science progresses towards the truth in a linear fashion, as older incorrect ideas get replaced by newer, correct ones. Later theories are thus objectively better than earlier ones. This 'cumulative' conception of science is popular among laymen and scientists alike, but Kuhn argued that it is both historically inaccurate and philosophically naïve. For example, he noted that Einstein's theory of relativity is in some respects more similar to Aristotelian than Newtonian theory – so the history of mechanics is not simply a linear progression from wrong to right. Moreover, Kuhn questioned whether the concept of objective truth actually makes sense at all. The idea that there is a fixed set of facts about the world, independent of any particular paradigm, was of dubious coherence, he believed. Kuhn suggested a radical alternative: the facts about the world are paradigm-relative, and thus change when paradigms change. If this suggestion is right, then it makes no sense to ask whether a given theory corresponds to the facts 'as they really are', nor therefore to ask whether it is objectively true. Truth itself becomes relative to a paradigm.

Incommensurability and the theory-ladenness of data

Kuhn had two main philosophical arguments for these claims. Firstly, he argued that competing paradigms are typically 'incommensurable' with one another. To understand this idea, we must remember that for Kuhn a scientist's paradigm determines her entire world-view – she views everything through the paradigm's lens. So when an existing paradigm is replaced by a new one in a scientific revolution, scientists have to abandon the whole conceptual framework which they use to make sense of the world. Indeed, Kuhn even claims, obviously somewhat metaphorically, that before and after a paradigm shift scientists 'live in different worlds'. Incommensurability is the idea that two paradigms may be so different as to render impossible any straightforward comparison of them with each other – there is no common language into which both can be translated. As a result, the proponents of different paradigms 'fail to make complete contact with each other's viewpoints', Kuhn claimed.

This is an interesting if somewhat vague idea. The doctrine of incommensurability stems largely from Kuhn's belief that scientific concepts derive their meaning from the theory in which they play a role. So to understand Newton's concept of mass, for example, we need to understand the whole of Newtonian theory – concepts cannot be explained independently of the theories in which they are embedded. This idea, which is sometimes called 'holism', was taken very seriously by Kuhn. He argued that the term 'mass' actually meant something different for Newton and Einstein, since the theories in which each embedded the term were so different. This implies that Newton and Einstein were in effect speaking different languages, which obviously complicates the attempt to choose between their theories. If a Newtonian and an Einsteinian physicist tried to have a rational discussion, they would end up talking past each other.

Kuhn used the incommensurability thesis both to rebut the view that paradigm shifts are fully 'objective', and to bolster his non-cumulative picture of the history of science. Traditional philosophy of science saw no huge difficulty in choosing between competing theories – you simply make an objective comparison of them, in the light of the available evidence, and decide which is better. But this clearly presumes that there is a common language in which both theories can be expressed. If Kuhn is right that proponents of old and new paradigms are quite literally talking past each other, no such simplistic account of paradigm choice can be correct. Incommensurability is equally problematic for the traditional 'linear' picture of scientific history. If old and new paradigms are incommensurable, then it cannot be correct to think of scientific revolutions as the replacement of 'wrong' ideas by 'right' ones. For to call one idea right and another wrong implies the existence of a common framework for evaluating them, which is precisely what Kuhn denies. Incommensurability implies that scientific change, far from being a straightforward progression towards the truth, is in a sense directionless: later paradigms are not better than earlier ones, just different.

Not many philosophers were convinced by Kuhn's incommensurability thesis. Part of the problem was that Kuhn also claimed old and new paradigms to be *incompatible*. This claim is very plausible, for if old and new paradigms were not incompatible there would be no need to choose between them. And in many cases the incompatibility is obvious – the Ptolemaic claim that the planets revolve around the earth is obviously incompatible with the Copernican claim that they revolve around the sun. But as Kuhn's critics were quick to point out, if two things are incommensurable then they cannot be incompatible. To see why not, consider the proposition that an object's mass depends on its velocity. Einstein's theory says this proposition is true while Newton's says it is false.

But if the doctrine of incommensurability is right, then there is no actual disagreement between Newton and Einstein here, for the proposition means something different for each. Only if the proposition has the *same* meaning in both theories, i.e. only if there is no incommensurability, is there a genuine conflict between the two. Since everybody (including Kuhn) agrees that Einstein's and Newton's theories do conflict, that is strong reason to regard the incommensurability thesis with suspicion.

In response to objections of this type, Kuhn moderated his incommensurability thesis somewhat. He insisted that even if two paradigms were incommensurable, that did not mean it was impossible to compare them with each other; it only made comparison more difficult. *Partial* translation between different paradigms could be achieved, Kuhn argued, so the proponents of old and new paradigms could communicate to some extent: they would not always be talking past each other entirely. But Kuhn continued to maintain that fully objective choice between paradigms was impossible. For in addition to the incommensurability deriving from the lack of a common language, there is also what he called 'incommensurability of standards'. This is the idea that proponents of different paradigms may disagree about the standards for evaluating paradigms, about which problems a good paradigm should solve, about what an acceptable solution to those problems would look like, and so on. So even if they can communicate effectively, they will not be able to reach agreement about whose paradigm is superior. In Kuhn's words, 'each paradigm will be shown to satisfy the criteria that it dictates for itself and to fall short of a few of those dictated by its opponent'.

Kuhn's second philosophical argument was based on an idea known as the 'theory-ladenness' of data. To grasp this idea, suppose you are a scientist trying to choose between two conflicting theories. The obvious thing to do is to look for a piece of data that will decide between the two – which is just what traditional philosophy of science recommended. But this will only be possible if there exist data that are suitably independent of the theories, in the sense that a scientist would accept the data whichever of the two theories she believed. As we have seen, the logical positivists believed in the existence of such theory-neutral data, which could provide an objective court of appeal between competing theories. But Kuhn argued that the ideal of theory-neutrality is an illusion – data are invariably contaminated by theoretical assumptions. It is impossible to isolate a set of 'pure' data which all scientists would accept irrespective of their theoretical persuasion.

The theory-ladenness of data had two important consequences for Kuhn. Firstly, it meant that the issue between competing paradigms could not be resolved by simply appealing to 'the data' or 'the facts', for what a scientist counts as data, or facts, will depend on which paradigm she accepts. Perfectly objective choice between two paradigms is therefore impossible: there is no neutral vantage-point from which to assess the claims of each. Secondly, the very idea of objective truth is called into question. For to be objectively true, our theories or beliefs must correspond to the facts, but the idea of such a correspondence makes little sense if the facts themselves are infected by our theories. This is why Kuhn was led to the radical view that truth itself is relative to a paradigm.

Why did Kuhn think that all data are theory-laden? His writings are not totally clear on this point, but at least two lines of argument are discernible. The first is the idea that perception is heavily conditioned by background beliefs – what we see depends in part on what we believe. So a trained scientist looking at a sophisticated piece of apparatus in a laboratory will see something different from what a layman sees, for the scientist obviously has many beliefs about the apparatus that the layman lacks. There are a number of psychological experiments that supposedly show that perception is sensitive in this way to background belief – though the correct interpretation of these experiments is a contentious matter. Secondly, scientists' experimental and observational reports are often couched in highly theoretical language. For example, a scientist might report the outcome of an experiment by saying 'an electric current is flowing through the copper rod'. But this data report is obviously laden with a large amount of theory. It would not be accepted by a scientist who did not hold standard beliefs about electric currents, so it is clearly not theory-neutral.

Philosophers are divided over the merits of these arguments. On the one hand, many agree with Kuhn that pure theory-neutrality is an unattainable ideal. The positivists' idea of a class of data statements totally free of theoretical commitment is rejected by most contemporary philosophers – not least because no-one has succeeded in saying what such statements would look like. But it is not clear that this compromises the objectivity of paradigm shifts altogether. Suppose, for example, that a Ptolemaic and a Copernican astronomer are engaged in a debate about whose theory is superior. In order for them to debate meaningfully, there needs to be some astronomical data they can agree on. But why should this be a problem? Surely they can agree about the relative position of the earth and the moon on successive nights, for example, or the time at which the sun rises? Obviously, if the Copernican insists on describing the data in a way that presumes the truth of the heliocentric theory, the Ptolemaist will object. But there is no reason why the Copernican should do that. Statements such as 'on May 14th the sun rose at 7.10 a.m.' can be agreed on by a scientist whether they believe the geocentric or the heliocentric theory. Such statements may not be *totally* theory-neutral, but they are sufficiently free of theoretical contamination to be acceptable to proponents of both paradigms, which is what matters.

It is even less obvious that the theory-ladenness of data forces us to abandon the concept of objective truth. Many philosophers would accept that theory-ladenness makes it hard to see how *knowledge* of objective truth is possible, but that is not to say that the very concept is incoherent. Part of the problem is that, like many people who are suspicious of the concept of objective truth, Kuhn failed to articulate a viable alternative. The radical view that truth is paradigm-relative is ultimately hard to make sense of. For like all such relativist doctrines, it faces a critical problem. Consider the question: is the claim that truth is paradigm-relative *itself* objectively true or not? If the proponent of relativism answers 'yes', then they have admitted that the concept of objective truth does make sense and have thus contradicted themselves. If they answer 'no', then they have no grounds on which to argue with someone who disagrees and says that, in their opinion, truth is *not* paradigm-relative. Not all philosophers regard this argument as completely fatal to relativism, but it does suggest that abandoning the concept of objective truth is easier said than done. Kuhn certainly raised some telling objections to the traditional view that the history of science is simply a linear progression to the truth, but the relativist alternative he offered in its place is far from unproblematic.

Kuhn and the rationality of science

The Structure of Scientific Revolutions is written in a very radical tone. Kuhn gives every impression of wanting to replace standard philosophical ideas about theory change in science with a totally new conception. His doctrine of paradigm shifts, of incommensurability, and of the theory-ladenness of data seems wholly at odds with the positivist view of science as a rational, objective, and cumulative enterprise. With much justification, most of Kuhn's early readers took him to be saying that science is an entirely non-rational activity, one characterized by dogmatic adherence to a paradigm in normal periods, and sudden 'conversion experiences' in revolutionary periods.

But Kuhn himself was unhappy with this interpretation of his work. In a Postscript to the second edition of *The Structure of Scientific Revolutions* published in 1970, and in subsequent writings, Kuhn moderated his tone considerably – and accused some of his early readers of having misread his intentions. His book was not an attempt to cast doubt on the rationality of science, he argued, but rather to offer a more realistic, historically accurate picture of how science actually develops. By neglecting the history of science, the positivists had been led to an excessively simplistic, indeed idealistic, account of how science works, and Kuhn's aim was simply to provide a corrective. He was not trying to show that science was irrational, but rather to provide a better account of what scientific rationality involves.

Some commentators regard Kuhn's Postscript as simply an about-turn – a retreat from his original position, rather than a clarification of it. Whether this is a fair assessment is not a question we will go into here. But the Postscript did bring to light one important issue. In rebutting the charge that he had portrayed paradigm shifts as non-rational, Kuhn made the famous claim that there is 'no algorithm' for theory choice in science. What does this mean? An algorithm is of a set of rules that allows us to compute the answer to a particular question. For example, an algorithm for multiplication is a set of rules that when applied to any two numbers tells us their product. (When you learn arithmetic in primary school, you in effect learn algorithms for addition, subtraction, multiplication, and division.) So an algorithm for theory choice is a set of rules that when applied to two competing theories would tell us which we should choose. Much positivist philosophy of science was in effect committed to the existence of such an algorithm. The positivists often wrote as if, given a set of data and two competing theories, the 'principles of scientific method' could be used to determine which theory was superior. This idea was implicit in their belief that although discovery was a matter of psychology, justification was a matter of logic.

Kuhn's insistence that there is no algorithm for theory choice in science is almost certainly correct. For no-one has ever succeeded in producing such an algorithm. Lots of philosophers and scientists have made plausible suggestions about what to look for in theories – simplicity, broadness of scope, close fit with the data, and so on. But these suggestions fall far short of providing a true algorithm, as Kuhn knew well. For one thing, there may be trade-offs: theory one may be simpler than theory two, but theory two may fit the data more closely. So an element of subjective judgement, or scientific common-sense, will often be needed to decide between competing theories. Seen in this light Kuhn's suggestion that the adoption of a new paradigm involves a certain act of faith does not seem quite so radical, and likewise his emphasis on the persuasiveness of a paradigm's advocates in determining its chance of winning over the scientific community.

The thesis that there is no algorithm for theory choice lends support to the view that Kuhn's account of paradigm shifts is not an assault on the rationality of science. For we can read Kuhn instead as rejecting a certain conception of rationality. The positivists believed, in effect, that there *must* be an algorithm for theory choice on pain of scientific change being irrational. This is by no means a crazy view: many paradigm cases of rational action do involve rules, or algorithms. For example, if you want to decide whether a good is cheaper in England or Japan, you apply an algorithm for converting pounds into yen; any other way of trying to decide the matter is irrational. Similarly, if a scientist is trying to decide between two competing theories, it is tempting to think that the only rational way to proceed is to apply an algorithm for theory choice. So if it turns out that there is no such algorithm, as seems likely, we have two options. Either we can conclude that scientific change is irrational *or* that the positivist conception of rationality is too demanding. In the Postscript Kuhn suggests that the latter is the correct reading of his work. The moral of his story is not that paradigm shifts are irrational, but rather that a more relaxed, non-algorithmic concept of rationality is required to make sense of them.

Kuhn's legacy

Despite their controversial nature, Kuhn's ideas transformed philosophy of science. In part this is because Kuhn called into question many assumptions that had traditionally been taken for granted, forcing philosophers to confront them, and in part because he drew attention to a range of issues that traditional philosophy of science had simply ignored. After Kuhn, the idea that philosophers could afford to ignore the history of science appeared increasingly untenable, as did the idea of a sharp dichotomy between the contexts of discovery and justification. Contemporary philosophers of science pay much greater attention to the historical development of science than did their pre-Kuhnian ancestors. Even those unsympathetic to Kuhn's more radical ideas would accept that in these respects his influence has been positive.

Another important impact of Kuhn's work was to focus attention on the social context in which science takes place, something that traditional philosophy of science ignored. Science for Kuhn is an intrinsically social activity: the existence of a scientific community, bound together by allegiance to a shared paradigm, is a pre-requisite for the practice of normal science. Kuhn also paid considerable attention to how science is taught in schools and universities, how young scientists are initiated into the scientific community, how scientific results are published, and other such 'sociological' matters. Not surprisingly, Kuhn's ideas have been very influential among sociologists of science. In particular, a movement known as the 'strong programme' in the sociology of science, which emerged in Britain in the 1970s, owed much to Kuhn.

The strong programme was based around the idea that science should be viewed as a product of the society in which it is practised. Strong programme sociologists took this idea very literally: they held that scientists' beliefs were in large part socially determined. So to explain why a scientist believes a given theory, for example, they would cite aspects of the scientist's social and cultural background. The scientist's own reasons for believing the theory were never explanation enough, they maintained. The strong programme borrowed a number of themes from Kuhn, including the theory-ladenness of data, the view of science as an essentially social enterprise, and the idea that there is no algorithm for theory choice. But strong programme sociologists were more radical than Kuhn, and less cautious. They openly rejected the notions of objective truth and rationality, which they regarded as ideologically suspect, and viewed traditional philosophy of science with great suspicion. This led to a certain amount of tension between philosophers and sociologists of science, which continues to this day.

Further afield, Kuhn's work has played a role in the rise of *cultural relativism* in the humanities and social sciences. Cultural relativism is not a precisely defined doctrine, but the central idea is that there is no such thing as absolute truth – truth is always relative to a particular culture. We may think that Western science reveals the truth about the world, but cultural relativists would say that other cultures and societies, for example indigenous Americans, have their own truth. As we have seen, Kuhn did indeed embrace relativist ideas. However, there is actually a certain irony in his having influenced cultural relativism. For cultural relativists are normally very anti-science. They object to the exalted status that science is accorded in our society, arguing that it discriminates against alternative belief systems that are equally valuable. But Kuhn himself was strongly pro-science. Like the positivists, he regarded modern science as a hugely impressive intellectual achievement. His doctrine of paradigm shifts, of normal and revolutionary science, of incommensurability and of theory-ladenness was not intended to undermine or criticize the scientific enterprise, but rather to help us understand it better.

Chapter 6
Philosophical problems in physics, biology, and psychology

The issues we have studied so far – induction, explanation, realism, and scientific change – belong to what is called 'general philosophy of science'. These issues concern the nature of scientific investigation in general, rather than pertaining specifically to chemistry, say, or geology. However, there are also many interesting philosophical questions that are specific to particular sciences – they belong to what is called 'philosophy of the special sciences'. These questions usually depend partly on philosophical considerations and partly on empirical facts, which is what makes them so interesting. In this chapter we examine three such questions, one each from physics, biology, and psychology.

Leibniz versus Newton on absolute space

Our first topic is a debate between Gottfried Leibniz (1646–1716) and Isaac Newton (1642–1727), two of the outstanding scientific intellects of the 17th century, concerning the nature of space and time. We shall focus primarily on space, but the issues about time are closely parallel. In his famous *Principles of Natural Philosophy*, Newton defended what is called an 'absolutist' conception of space. According to this view, space has an 'absolute' existence over and above the spatial relations between objects. Newton thought of space as a three-dimensional container into which God had placed the material universe at creation. This implies that space existed before there were any material objects, just as a container like a cereal box exists before any pieces of cereal are put inside. The only difference between space and ordinary containers like cereal boxes, according to Newton, is that the latter obviously have finite dimensions, whereas space extends infinitely in every direction.

Leibniz strongly disagreed with the absolutist view of space, and with much else in Newton's philosophy. He argued that space consists simply of the totality of spatial relations between material objects. Examples of spatial relations are 'above', 'below', 'to the left of', and 'to the right of' – they are relations that material objects bear to each other. This 'relationist' conception of space implies that before there were any material objects, space did not exist. Leibniz argued that space came into existence *when* God created the material universe; it did not exist beforehand, waiting to be filled up with material objects. So space is not usefully thought of as a container, nor indeed as an entity of any sort. Leibniz's view can be understood in terms of an analogy. A legal contract consists of a relationship between two parties – the buyer and seller of a house, for example. If one of the parties dies, then the contract ceases to exist. So it would be crazy to say that the contract has an existence independently of the relationship between buyer and seller – the contract just *is* that relationship. Similarly, space is nothing over and above the spatial relations between objects.

Newton's main reason for introducing the concept of absolute space was to distinguish between absolute and relative motion. Relative motion is the motion of one object with respect to another. So far as relative motion is concerned, it makes no sense to ask whether an object is 'really' moving or not – we can only ask whether it is moving with respect to some other object. To illustrate, imagine two joggers running in tandem along a straight road. Relative to a by-stander standing on the roadside, both are obviously in motion:

they are getting further away by the moment. But relative to each other, the joggers are not in motion: their relative positions remain exactly the same, so long as they keep jogging in the same direction at the same speed. So an object may be in relative motion with respect to one thing but be stationary with respect to another.

Newton believed that as well as relative motion, there is also absolute motion. Common-sense supports this view. For intuitively, it *does* make sense to ask whether an object is 'really' moving or not. Imagine two objects in relative motion – say a hang-glider and an observer on the earth. Now relative motion is symmetric: just as the hang-glider is in motion relative to the observer on the earth, so the observer is in motion relative to the hang-glider. But surely it makes sense to ask whether the observer or the hang-glider is 'really' moving, or both? If that is so, then we need the concept of absolute motion.

But what exactly *is* absolute motion? According to Newton, it is the motion of an object *with respect to absolute space itself.* Newton thought that at any time, every object has a particular location in absolute space. If an object changes its location in absolute space from one time to another then it is in absolute motion; otherwise, it is at absolute rest. So we need to think of space as an absolute entity, over and above the relations between material objects, in order to distinguish relative from absolute motion. Notice that Newton's reasoning rests on an important assumption. He assumes without question that all motion has got to be relative to something. Relative motion is motion relative to other material objects; absolute motion is motion relative to absolute space itself. So in a sense, even absolute motion is 'relative' for Newton. In effect, Newton is assuming that being in motion, whether absolute or relative, cannot be a 'brute fact' about an object; it can only be a fact about the object's relations to something else. That something else can either be another material object, or it can be absolute space.

Leibniz accepted that there was a difference between relative and absolute motion, but he denied that the latter should be explained as motion with respect to absolute space. For he regarded the concept of absolute space as incoherent. He had a number of arguments for this view, many of which were theological in nature. From a philosophical point of view, Leibniz's most interesting argument was that absolute space conflicts with what he called the principle of the identity of indiscernibles (PII). Since Leibniz regarded this principle as indubitably true, he rejected the concept of absolute space.

PII says that if two objects are indiscernible, then they are identical, i.e. they are really one and the same object. What does it mean to call two objects indiscernible? It means that no difference at all can be found between them – they have exactly the same attributes. So if PII is true, then any two genuinely distinct objects must differ in at least one of their attributes – otherwise they would be one, not two. PII is intuitively quite compelling. It certainly is not easy to find an example of two distinct objects that share *all* their attributes. Even two mass-produced factory goods will normally differ in innumerable ways, even if the differences cannot be detected with the naked eye. Whether PII is true in general is a complex question that philosophers still debate; the answer depends in part on exactly what counts as an 'attribute', and in part on difficult issues in quantum physics. But our concern for the moment is the use to which Leibniz puts the principle.

Leibniz uses two thought experiments to reveal a conflict between Newton's theory of absolute space and PII. His argumentative strategy is indirect: he assumes for the sake of argument that Newton's theory is correct, then tries to show that a contradiction follows from that assumption; since contradictions cannot be true, Leibniz concludes that Newton's theory must be false. Recall that for Newton, at any moment in time every object in the universe has a definite location in absolute space. Leibniz asks us to imagine two different universes, both containing exactly the same objects. In universe one, each object occupies a particular location in absolute space. In universe two, each object has been shifted to a different location in absolute space, two miles to the east (for example). There would be no way of telling these two universes apart. For we cannot observe the position of an object in absolute space, as Newton himself admitted. All we can observe are the positions of objects *relative to each other*, and these would remain unchanged – for all objects are shifted by the same amount. No observations or experiments could ever reveal whether we lived in universe one or two.

The second thought experiment is similar. Recall that for Newton, some objects are moving through absolute space while others are at rest. This means that at each moment, every object has a definite absolute velocity. (Velocity is speed in a given direction, so an object's absolute velocity is the speed at which it moves through absolute space in a specified direction. Objects at absolute rest have an absolute velocity of zero.) Now imagine two different universes, both containing exactly the same objects. In universe one, each object has a particular absolute velocity. In universe two, the absolute velocity of each object has been boosted by a fixed amount, say 300 kilometres per hour in a specified direction. Again, we could never tell these two universes apart. For it is impossible to observe how fast an object is moving with respect to absolute space, as Newton himself admitted. We can only observe how fast objects are moving *relative to each other* – and these relative velocities would remain unchanged, for the velocity of every object is boosted by exactly the same amount. No observations or experiments could ever reveal whether we lived in universe one or two.

In each of these thought experiments, Leibniz describes two universes which by Newton's own admission we could never tell apart – they are perfectly indiscernible. But by PII, this means that the two universes are actually one. So it follows that Newton's theory of absolute space is false. Another way to see the point is this. Newton's theory implies that there is a genuine difference between the universe being at one location in absolute space and it being shifted to a different location. But Leibniz points out that this difference would be totally undetectable, so long as every object shifts location by the same amount. But if no difference can be detected between two universes then they are indiscernible, and PII tells us that they are actually the same universe. So Newton's theory has a false consequence: it implies that there are two things when there is only one. The concept of absolute space thus conflicts with PII. The logic of Leibniz's second thought experiment is identical.

In effect, Leibniz is arguing that absolute space is an empty notion, because it makes no observational difference. If neither the location of objects in absolute space nor their velocity with respect to absolute space can ever be detected, why believe in absolute space at all? Leibniz is appealing to the quite reasonable principle that we should only postulate unobservable entities in science if their existence would make a difference that we can detect observationally.

But Newton thought he could show that absolute space *did* have observational effects. This is the point of his famous 'rotating bucket' argument. He asks us to imagine a bucket full of water, suspended by a rope through a hole attached to its base (Figure 12).

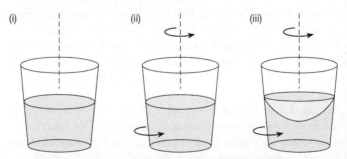

12. Newton's 'rotating bucket' experiment. In stage (i) bucket and water are at rest; in stage (ii) the bucket rotates relative to the water; in stage (iii) bucket and water rotate in tandem.

Initially the water is at rest relative to the bucket. Then the rope is twisted around a number of times and released. As it uncoils, the bucket starts rotating. At first the water in the bucket stays still, its surface flat; the bucket is then rotating relative to the water. But after a few moments the bucket imparts its motion to the water, and the water begins to rotate in tandem with the bucket; the bucket and the water are then at rest relative to each other again. Experience shows that the surface of the water then curves upwards at the sides, as the diagram indicates.

What is causing the surface of the water to rise?, Newton asks. Clearly it is something to do with the water's rotation. But rotation is a type of motion, and for Newton an object's motion is always relative to something else. So we must ask: relative to what is the water rotating? Not relative to the bucket, obviously, for the bucket and the water are rotating in tandem and are hence at relative rest. Newton argues that the water is rotating relative to absolute space, and that this is causing its surface to curve upwards. So absolute space does in fact have observational effects.

You may think there is an obvious gap in Newton's argument. Granted the water is not rotating relative to the bucket, but why conclude that it must be rotating relative to absolute space? The water is rotating relative to the person doing the experiment, and relative to the earth's surface, and relative to the fixed stars, so surely any of these might be causing its surface to rise? But Newton had a simple response to this move. Imagine a universe containing nothing except the rotating bucket. In such a universe, we cannot explain the water's curved surface by appealing to the water's rotation relative to other objects, for there are none, and as before the water is at rest relative to the bucket. Absolute space is the only thing left for the water to be rotating relative to. So we must believe in absolute space on pain of being unable to explain why the water's surface curves.

In effect, Newton is saying that although an object's position in absolute space and its velocity with respect to absolute space can never be detected, it *is* possible to tell when an object is *accelerating* with respect to absolute space. For when an object rotates then it is by definition accelerating, even if the rate of rotation is constant. This is because in physics, acceleration is defined as the rate of change of velocity, and velocity is speed *in a fixed direction*. Since rotating objects are constantly changing their direction of motion, it follows that their velocity is not constant, hence they are accelerating. The water's curved surface is just one example of what are called 'inertial effects' – effects produced by accelerated motion. Another example is the feeling of being pushed to the back of your seat that you get when an aeroplane takes off. The only possible explanation of inertial effects, Newton believed, is the acceleration of the object experiencing those effects with respect to absolute space. For in a universe containing only the accelerating object, absolute space is the only thing that the acceleration could be relative to.

Newton's argument is powerful but not conclusive. For how does Newton know that the water's surface *would* curve upwards, if the rotating bucket experiment was done in a universe containing no other material objects? Newton simply assumes that the inertial effects we find in this world would remain the same in a world bereft of any other matter. This is obviously quite a substantial assumption, and many people have questioned Newton's entitlement to it. So Newton's argument does not prove the existence of absolute space. Rather, it lays down a challenge to the defender of Leibniz to provide an alternative explanation of inertial effects.

Leibniz also faces the challenge of explaining the difference between absolute and relative motion without invoking absolute space. On this problem, Leibniz wrote that a body is in true or absolute motion 'when the immediate cause of the change is in the body itself'. Recall the case of the hang-glider and the observer on earth, both of whom are in motion relative to the other. To determine which is 'really' moving, Leibniz would say that we need to decide whether the immediate cause of the change (i.e. of the relative motion) is in the hang-glider, the observer, or both. This suggestion for how to distinguish absolute from relative motion avoids all reference to absolute space, but it is not very clear. Leibniz never properly explains what it *means* for the 'immediate cause of the change' to be in an object. But it may be that he intended to reject Newton's assumption that an object's motion, whether relative or absolute, can only be a fact about the object's relations to something else.

One of the intriguing things about the absolute/relational controversy is that it refuses to go away. Newton's account of space was intimately bound up with his physics, and Leibniz's views were a direct reaction to Newton's. So one might think that the advances in physics since the 17th century would have resolved the issue by now. But this has not happened. Although it was once widely held that Einstein's theory of relativity had decided the issue in favour of Leibniz, this view has increasingly come under attack in recent years. More than 300 years after the original Newton/Leibniz debate, the controversy rages on.

The problem of biological classification

Classifying, or sorting the objects one is studying into general kinds, plays a role in every science. Geologists classify rocks as igneous, sedimentary, or metamorphic, depending on how they were formed. Economists classify taxation systems as proportional, progressive, or regressive, depending on how unfair they are. The main function of classification is to convey information. If a chemist tells you that something is a metal, that tells you a lot about its likely behaviour. Classification raises some interesting philosophical issues. Mostly, these stem from the fact that any given set of objects can in principle be classified in many different ways. Chemists classify substances by their atomic number, yielding the periodic table of the elements. But they could equally classify substances by their colour, or their smell, or their density. So how should we choose between these alternative ways of classifying? Is there a 'correct' way to classify? Or are all classification schemes ultimately arbitrary? These questions take on a particular urgency in the context of biological classification, or taxonomy, which will be our concern here.

Biologists traditionally classify plants and organisms using the Linnean system, named after the 18th-century Swedish naturalist Carl Linnaeus (1707–1778) (Figure 13). The basic elements of the Linnean system are straightforward, and familiar to many people. First of all, individual organisms are assigned to a *species*. Each species is then assigned to a *genus*, each genus to a *family*, each family to an *order*, each order to a *class*, each class to a *phylum*, and each phylum to a *kingdom*. Various intermediate ranks, such as *subspecies*, *subfamily*, and *superfamily* are also recognized. The species is the base taxonomic unit; genuses, families, orders, and so on are known as 'higher taxa'. The standard Latin name for a species indicates the genus to which the species belongs, but no more. For example, you and I belong to *Homo sapiens*, the only surviving species in the Homo genus. Two of the other species in that genus are *Homo erectus* and *Homo habilis*, both now extinct. The Homo genus belongs to the Hominid family, which belongs to the Hominoid superfamily, which belongs to the Primate order, which belongs to the Mammalian class, which belongs to the Chordate phylum, which belongs to the Animal kingdom.

Notice that the Linnean way of classifying organisms is hierarchical: a number of species are nested in a single genus, a number of genuses in a single family, a number of families in a single order, and so on. So as we move upwards, we find fewer taxa at each level. At the bottom there are literally millions of species, but at the top there are just five kingdoms: Animals, Plants, Fungi, Bacteria, and Protoctists (algae, seaweed, etc.). Not every classification system in science is hierarchical. The periodic table in

CAROLI LINNÆI

Naturæ Curioforum *Diofcoridis Secundi*

SYSTEMA
NATURÆ

IN QUO

NATURÆ REGNA TRIA,

SECUNDUM.

CLASSES, ORDINES, GENERA, SPECIES,

SYSTEMATICE PROPONUNTUR,

Editio Secunda, Auctior.

STOCKHOLMIÆ

Apud GOTTFR. KIESEWETTER.

1740.

13. Linneaus' most famous book *Systema Naturae*, in which he presented his classification of plants, animals, and minerals.

chemistry is an example of a non-hierarchical classification. The different chemical elements are not arranged into more and more inclusive groupings, the way species are in the Linnean system. One important question we must face is *why* biological classification should be hierarchical.

The Linnean system served naturalists well for hundreds of years, and continues to be used today. In some ways this is surprising, since biological theories have changed greatly in that period. The cornerstone of modern biology is Darwin's theory of evolution, which says that contemporary species have descended from ancestral species; this theory contrasts with the older, biblically inspired view that each species was created separately by God. Darwin's *Origin of Species* was published in 1859, but it was not until the middle of the 20th century that biologists began to ask whether the theory of evolution should have any impact on the way organisms are classified. By the 1970s two rival taxonomic schools had emerged, offering competing answers to this question. According to *cladists*, biological classifications should try to reflect the evolutionary relationships between species, so knowledge of evolutionary history is indispensable for doing good taxonomy. According to *pheneticists*, this is not so: classification can and should be totally independent of evolutionary considerations. A third group, known as the *evolutionary taxonomists*, try to combine elements of both views.

To understand the dispute between cladists and pheneticists, we must divide the problem of biological classification into two. Firstly, there is the problem of how to sort organisms into species, known as the 'species problem'. This problem has by no means been solved, but in practice biologists are often able to agree about how to delimit species, though there are difficult cases. Broadly speaking, biologists assign organisms to the same species if they can interbreed with each other and to different species otherwise. Secondly, there is the problem of how to arrange a group of species into higher taxa, which obviously presumes a solution to the first problem. As it happens, cladists and pheneticists do often disagree about the species problem, but their dispute primarily concerns higher taxa. So for the moment, we ignore the species problem – we assume that organisms have been allocated to species in a satisfactory way. The question is: where do we go from there? What principles do we use to classify these species into higher taxa?

To focus the issue, consider the following example. Humans, chimpanzees, gorillas, bonobos, orangutans, and gibbons are usually classed together as members of the Hominoid superfamily. But baboons are not counted as Hominoids. Why is this? What is the justification for placing humans, chimps, gorillas, etc. in a group that doesn't also contain baboons? According to pheneticists, the answer is that the former all have a number of features that baboons do not, for example the lack of a tail. On this view, taxonomic groupings should be based on *similarity* – they should bring together species that are similar to each other in important ways and leave out ones that are dissimilar. Intuitively, this is a reasonable view. For it fits neatly with the idea that the purpose of classification is to convey information. If taxonomic groups are based on similarity, then being told which group a particular organism belongs to will tell you a lot about its likely characteristics. If you are told that a given organism belongs to the Hominoid superfamily, you will know that it doesn't have a tail. Furthermore, many of the groups recognized by traditional taxonomy do seem to be similarity-based. To take an obvious example, plants all share a number of features that animals lack, so placing all the plants in one kingdom and all the animals in another makes good sense from the phenetic point of view.

However, cladists insist that similarity should count for nothing in classification. Rather what matters are the evolutionary relationships between species – known as their *phylogenetic* relations. Cladists agree that the baboons should be excluded from the group that contains humans, chimps, gorillas, etc. But the justification for this has got nothing to do with the similarities and dissimilarities between the species. The point is rather that the Hominoid species are more closely related to each other than are any of them to the baboons. What exactly does this mean? It means that all of the Hominoid species share a common ancestor that is not an ancestor of the baboons. Notice that this does *not* mean that the Hominoid species and the baboons have no common ancestor at all. On the contrary, any two species have a common ancestor if you go back far enough in evolutionary time – for all life on earth is presumed to have a single origin. The point is rather that the common ancestor of the Hominoid species and the baboons is also an ancestor of many other species, for example the various macaque species. So cladists argue that any taxonomic group that contains the Hominoid species and the baboons must also contain these other species. No taxonomic group can contain *just* the Hominoid species and the baboons.

The key cladistic idea is that all taxonomic groups, be they genuses, families, superfamilies, or whatever, must be *monophyletic*. A monophyletic group is one that contains an ancestral species and all of its descendants, but no-one else. Monophyletic groups come in various sizes. At one extreme, all species that have ever existed form a monophyletic group, presuming life on earth only originated once. At the other extreme, there can be monophyletic groups of just two species – if they are the only descendants of a common ancestor. The group that contains just the Hominoid species and the baboons is not monophyletic, for as we saw, the common ancestor of the Hominoid species and the baboons is also ancestral to the macaques. So it is not a genuine taxonomic group, according to cladists. Groups that are not monophyletic are not permitted in cladistic taxonomy, irrespective of how similar their members may be. For cladists regard such groupings as wholly artificial, by contrast with 'natural' monophyletic groups.

The concept of monophyly is easily understood graphically. Consider the diagram below – known as a *cladogram* – which shows the phylogenetic relationships between six contemporary species,

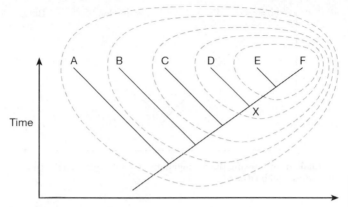

14. Cladogram showing the phylogenetic relations between six contemporary species.

A–F (Figure 14). All six species have a common ancestor if we go back far enough in time, but some are more closely related than others. Species E and F have a very recent common ancestor – for their branches intersect in the quite recent past. By contrast, species A split off from the rest of the lineage a long time ago. Now consider the group {D, E, F}. This is a monophyletic group, since it contains all and only the descendants of an ancestral species (not named), which split into two at the node marked 'x'. The group {C, D, E, F} is likewise monophyletic, as is the group {B, C, D, E, F}. But the group {B, C, D, F} is not monophyletic. This is because the common ancestor of these four species is also an ancestor of species E. All the monophyletic groups in the diagram have been ringed; any other group of species is not monophyletic.

The dispute between cladists and pheneticists is by no means purely academic – there are many real cases where they disagree. One well-known example concerns the class Reptilia, or the reptiles. Traditional Linnean taxonomy counts lizards and crocodiles as members of Reptilia, but excludes birds, which are placed in a separate class called Aves. Pheneticists agree with this traditional

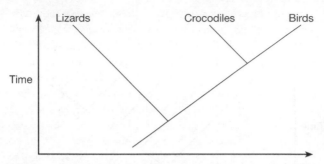

15. Cladogram showing the phylogenetic relations between lizards, crocodiles, and birds.

classification, for birds have their own unique anatomy and physiology, which is quite different from that of lizards, crocodiles, and other reptiles. But cladists maintain that Reptilia is not a genuine taxonomic group at all, for it is not monophyletic. As the cladogram above shows, the common ancestor of the lizards and the crocodiles is also an ancestor of the birds; so placing lizards and crocodiles together in a group that excludes birds violates the requirement of monophyly (Figure 15). Cladists therefore recommend that traditional taxonomic practice be abandoned: biologists should not talk about Reptilia at all, for it is an artificial not a natural group. This is quite a radical recommendation; even biologists sympathetic to the spirit of cladism are often reluctant to abandon the traditional taxonomic categories that have served naturalists well for centuries.

Cladists argue that their way of classifying is 'objective' while that of the pheneticists is not. There is certainly some truth in this charge. For pheneticists base their classifications on the similarities between species, and judgements of similarity are invariably partly subjective. Any two species are going to be similar to each other in some respects, but not in others. For example, two species of insect might be anatomically quite similar, but very diverse in their feeding habits. So which 'respects' do we single out, in order to make judgements of similarity? Pheneticists hoped to avoid this problem by defining a measure of 'overall similarity', which would take into account all of a species' characteristics, thus permitting fully objective classifications to be constructed. But though this idea sounds nice, it did not work, not least because there is no obvious way to count characteristics. Most people today believe that the very idea of 'overall similarity' is philosophically suspect. Phenetic classifications do exist, and are used in practice, but they are not fully objective. Different similarity judgements lead to different phenetic classifications, and there is no obvious way to choose between them.

Cladism faces its own set of problems. The most serious problem is that in order to construct a classification according to cladistic principles, we need to discover the phylogenetic relations between the species we are trying to classify, and this is very far from easy. These relations are obviously not discoverable just by looking at the species – they have to be inferred. A variety of techniques for inferring phylogenetic relations have been developed, but they are not fool-proof. Indeed, as more and more evidence from molecular genetics emerges, hypotheses about the phylogenetic relations between species get overturned rapidly. So actually putting cladistic ideas into practice is not easy. It is all very well to be told that only monophyletic groups of species are allowed in taxonomy, but this is of limited use unless one knows whether a given group *is* monophyletic or not. In effect, cladistic classifications constitute hypotheses about the phylogenetic relations between species, and are thus inherently conjectural. Pheneticists object that classification should not be theory-laden in this way. They maintain that taxonomy should be prior to, not dependent on, conjectures about evolutionary history.

Despite the difficulty of putting cladism into practice, and despite the fact the cladists often recommend quite radical revisions of traditional taxonomic categories, more and more biologists are coming round to the cladistic viewpoint. This is mainly because cladism is free of ambiguity in a way that phenetic and other approaches are not – its taxonomic principles are perfectly clear, even if they are hard to implement. And there is something quite intuitive about the idea that monophyletic groups of species are 'natural units', while other groups are not. Furthermore, cladism provides a genuine rationale for why biological classification should be hierarchical. As Figure 15 above indicates, monophyletic groups are always nested inside each other, so if the requirement of monophyly is rigidly followed the resulting classification will automatically be hierarchical. Classifying on the basis of similarity can also yield a hierarchical classification; but pheneticists have no comparable justification for *why* biological classification should be hierarchical. It is quite striking that naturalists have been classifying living organisms hierarchically for hundreds of years, but the true rationale for doing so has only recently become clear.

Is the mind modular?

One of the central jobs of psychology is to understand how human beings manage to perform the cognitive tasks they do. By 'cognitive tasks' we do not just mean things like solving crossword puzzles, but also more mundane tasks like crossing the road safely, understanding what other people say, recognizing other people's faces, checking one's change in a shop, and so on. There is no denying that humans are very good at many of these tasks – so good, indeed, that we often do them very fast, with little if any conscious thought. To appreciate just how remarkable this is, consider the fact that no robot has ever been designed that behaves even remotely like a human being in a real-life situation, despite considerable effort and expense. No robot can solve a crossword, or engage in a conversation, with anything like the facility the average human being can. Somehow or other, we humans are capable of performing complex cognitive tasks with minimal effort. Trying to understand how this could be is the central explanatory problem of the discipline known as cognitive psychology.

Our focus is an old but ongoing debate among cognitive psychologists concerning the architecture of the human mind. According to one view, the human mind is a 'general-purpose problem-solver'. This means that the mind contains a set of general problem-solving skills, or 'general intelligence', which it applies to an indefinitely large number of different tasks. So one and the same set of cognitive capacities is employed, whether the human is trying to count marbles, decide which restaurant to eat in, or learn a foreign language – these tasks represent different applications of the human's general intelligence. According to a rival view, the human mind contains a number of specialized subsystems or modules, each of which is designed for performing a very limited range of tasks and cannot do anything else (Figure 16). This is known as the *modularity of mind* hypothesis. So, for example, it is widely believed that there is a special module for language acquisition, a view deriving from the work of the linguist Noam Chomsky. Chomsky insisted that a child does not learn to speak by overhearing adult conversation and then using his 'general intelligence' to figure out the rules of the language being spoken; rather, there is a distinct 'language acquisition device' in every human child which operates automatically, and whose sole function is to enable him or her to learn a language, given appropriate prompting. Chomsky provided an array of impressive evidence for this claim – including, for example, the fact that even those with very low 'general intelligence' can often learn to speak perfectly well.

Some of the most compelling evidence for the modularity hypothesis comes from studies of patients with brain damage, known as 'deficit studies'. If the human mind is a general-purpose problem-solver, we would expect damage to the brain to affect all cognitive capacities more or less equally. But this is not what we find. On the contrary, brain damage often impairs some cognitive capacities but leaves others untouched. For example, damage to a part of the brain known as Wernicke's area leaves patients unable to understand speech, though they are still able to produce fluent,

113

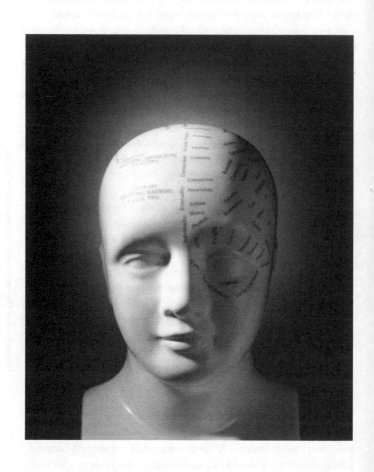

16. A hypothetical representation of a modular mind.

grammatical sentences. This strongly suggests that there are separate modules for sentence production and comprehension – for that would explain why loss of the latter capacity does not entail loss of the former. Other brain-damaged patients lose their long-term memory (amnesia), but their short-term memory and their ability to speak and understand are entirely unimpaired. Again, this seems to speak in favour of modularity and against the view of the mind as a general-purpose problem-solver.

Though compelling, neuropsychological evidence of this sort does not settle the modularity issue once and for all. For one thing, the evidence is relatively sparse – we obviously cannot damage people's brains at will just to see how their cognitive capacities are affected. In addition, there are serious disagreements about how the data should be interpreted, as is usual in science. Some people argue that the observed pattern of cognitive impairment in brain-damaged patients does not imply that the mind is modular. Even if the mind *were* a general-purpose problem-solver, that is non-modular, it is still possible that distinct cognitive capacities might be differentially affected by brain damage, they argue. So we cannot simply 'read off' the architecture of the mind from deficit studies, they maintain; at best, the latter provide fallible evidence for the former.

Much of the recent interest in modularity is due to the work of Jerry Fodor, an influential American philosopher and psychologist. In 1983 Fodor published a book called *The Modularity of Mind* which contained both a very clear account of what exactly a module is, and some interesting hypotheses about which cognitive capacities are modular and which not. Fodor argued that mental modules have a number of distinguishing features, of which the following three are the most important: (i) they are *domain-specific*, (ii) their operation is *mandatory*, and (iii) they are *informationally encapsulated*. Non-modular cognitive systems possess none of these features. Fodor then argued that the human mind is partly, though not wholly, modular: we solve some cognitive tasks using specialized modules, others using our 'general intelligence'.

To say that a cognitive system is domain-specific is to say that it is specialized: it performs a limited, precisely circumscribed set of tasks. Chomsky's postulated 'language acquisition device' is a good example of a domain-specific system. The sole function of this device is to enable the child to learn language – it doesn't help the child learn to play chess, or to count, or to do anything else. So the device simply ignores non-linguistic inputs. To say that a cognitive system is mandatory is to say that we cannot choose whether or not to put the system into operation. The perception of language provides a good example. If you hear a sentence uttered in a language you know, you cannot help but hear it as the utterance of a sentence. If someone asked you to hear the sentence as 'pure noise' you could not obey them however hard you tried. Fodor points out that not all cognitive processes are mandatory in this way. *Thinking* clearly is not. If someone asked you to think of the scariest moment in your life, or to think of what you would most like to do if you won the lottery, you clearly could obey their instructions. So thinking and language perception are quite different in this regard.

What about information encapsulation, the third and most crucial feature of mental modules? This notion is best illustrated by an example. Look at the two lines in Figure 17.

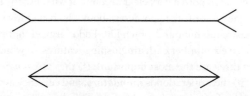

17. The Müller-Lyer illusion. The horizontal lines are equal in length, but the top one looks longer.

To most people, the top line looks slightly longer than the bottom one. But in fact this is an optical illusion, known as the Müller-Lyer illusion. The lines are actually equal in length. Various explanations have been suggested for why the top line looks longer, but they need not concern us here. The crucial point is this: the lines continue to look unequal in length, *even when you know it's an optical illusion*. According to Fodor, this simple fact has important implications for understanding the architecture of the mind. For it shows that the information that the two lines are equal in length is stored in a region of the cognitive mind to which our perceptual mechanisms do not have access. This means that our perceptual mechanisms are informationally encapsulated – they do not have access to all of the information we possess. If visual perception were not informationally encapsulated in this way, but could make use of all the information stored in the mind, then the illusion would disappear as soon as you were told that the lines were actually equal in length.

Another possible example of information encapsulation comes from the phenomenon of human phobias. Take, for example, odiophobia, or fear of snakes. This phobia is quite widespread in humans, and also in many other primate species. This is easily understood, for snakes are very dangerous to primates, so an instinctive fear of snakes could easily have evolved by natural selection. But whatever the explanation for why we are so scared of snakes, the crucial point is this. Even if you know that a particular snake isn't dangerous, for example because you've been told that its poison glands have been removed, you are still quite likely to be terrified of the snake and will not want to touch it. Of course, this sort of phobia can often be overcome by training, but that is a different matter. The relevant point is that the information that the snake isn't dangerous is inaccessible to the part of your mind that produces in you the reaction of fear when you see a snake. This suggests that there may be an inbuilt, informationally encapsulated 'fear of snakes' module in every human being.

You may wonder why the modularity of mind issue is at all philosophical. Surely it is just a question of empirical fact whether the mind is modular or not, albeit not an easy one to answer? In fact this suggestion is not quite right. One respect in which the modularity debate is philosophical concerns how we should count cognitive tasks and modules. Advocates of modularity hold that the mind contains specialized modules for performing different sorts of cognitive task; opponents of modularity deny this. But how do we decide whether two tasks are of the same sort, or of different sorts? Is facial recognition a single cognitive task or is it comprised of two distinct cognitive tasks: recognizing male faces and recognizing female faces? Are doing long division and doing multiplication different cognitive tasks, or are they both part of the more general task of doing arithmetic? Questions of this sort are conceptual or philosophical, rather than straightforwardly empirical, and they are potentially crucial to the modularity debate. For suppose an opponent of modularity produces some experimental evidence to show that we use one and the same set of cognitive capacities to perform many different types of cognitive task. Her opponent might accept the experimental data, but argue that the cognitive tasks in questions are all of the *same* type, and thus that the data are perfectly compatible with modularity. So first appearances to the contrary notwithstanding, the modularity of mind debate is up to its neck in philosophical issues.

The most enthusiastic advocates of modularity believe that the mind is entirely composed of modules, but this view is not widely accepted. Fodor himself argues that perception and language are probably modular, while thought and reasoning are almost certainly not. To see why not, suppose you are sitting on a jury and are trying to decide whether to return a verdict of guilty or not guilty. How will you go about your task? One important issue you will consider is whether the defendant's story is logically consistent or not – is it free from contradiction? And you will probably ask yourself whether the available evidence is merely compatible with the defendant's guilt or whether it strongly supports it. Clearly, the reasoning skills you apply here – testing for logical consistency and assessing evidence – are *general* skills; they are not specifically designed for use in jury service. You use the same skills in many domains. So the cognitive capacities you bring to bear in deliberating the defendant's guilt are not domain-specific. Nor is their operation mandatory – you have to consciously consider whether the defendant is guilty, and can stop doing so whenever you want to, e.g. during the lunch break. Most important of all, there is no information encapsulation either. Your task is to decide whether the defendant is guilty *all things considered*, so you may have to draw on any of the background information that you possess, if you consider it relevant. For example, if the defendant twitched nervously under cross-examination and you believe that nervous twitching is invariably a sign of guilt, you will probably draw on this belief in reaching your verdict. So there is no store of information which is inaccessible to the cognitive mechanisms you employ to reach your verdict (though the judge may tell you to ignore certain things). In short, there is no module for deciding whether a defendant is guilty. You tackle this cognitive problem using your 'general intelligence'.

Fodor's thesis that the mind is partly though not wholly modular thus looks quite plausible. But exactly how many modules there are, and what precisely they do, are questions that cannot be answered given the current state of research. Fodor himself is quite pessimistic about the possibility of cognitive psychology ever explaining the workings of the human mind. He believes that only modular systems can be studied scientifically – non-modular systems, because they are not informationally encapsulated, are much more difficult to model. So according to Fodor the best research strategy for cognitive psychologists is to focus on perception and language, ignoring thinking and reasoning. But this aspect of Fodor's thought is very controversial. Not all psychologists agree with him about which bits of the mind are modular and which are not, and not all agree that only modular systems can be studied scientifically.

Chapter 7
Science and its critics

Many people take it for granted that science is a good thing, for obvious reasons. After all, science has given us electricity, safe drinking water, penicillin, contraception, air travel, and much more – all of which have undoubtedly benefited humanity. But despite these impressive contributions to human welfare, science is not without its critics. Some argue that society spends too much money on science at the expense of the arts; others hold that science has given us technological capabilities we would be better off without, such as the capacity to produce weapons of mass destruction (Figure 18). Certain feminists argue that science is

18. Scientific capabilities we would be better off without: a toxic mushroom cloud produced by an atomic explosion.

objectionable because it is inherently male-biased; those of religious persuasion often feel that science threatens their faith; and anthropologists have accused Western science of arrogance, on the grounds that it blithely assumes its superiority to the knowledge and beliefs of indigenous cultures around the world. This by no means exhausts the list of criticisms to which science has been subject, but in this chapter we confine our attention to three that are of particular philosophical interest.

Scientism

The words 'science' and 'scientific' have acquired a peculiar cachet in modern times. If someone accuses you of behaving 'unscientifically', they are almost certainly criticizing you. Scientific conduct is sensible, rational, and praiseworthy; unscientific conduct is foolish, irrational, and worthy of contempt. It is difficult to know why the label 'scientific' should have acquired these connotations, but it is probably something to do with the high status in which science is held in modern society. Society treats scientists as experts, whose opinions are regularly sought on matters of importance and for the most part accepted without question. Of course, everybody recognizes that scientists sometimes get it wrong – for example, scientific advisers to the British government in the 1990s declared that 'mad cow disease' posed no threat to humans, only to be proved tragically mistaken. But occasional hiccups of this sort tend not to shake the faith that the public place in science, nor the esteem in which scientists are held. In the West at least, scientists are viewed much as religious leaders used to be: possessors of specialized knowledge that is inaccessible to the laity.

'Scientism' is a pejorative label used by some philosophers to describe what they see as science-worship – the over-reverential attitude towards science found in many intellectual circles. Opponents of scientism argue that science is not the only valid form of intellectual endeavour, and not the uniquely privileged route to knowledge. They often stress that they are not anti-science *per se*; what they are opposed to is the privileged status accorded to science, particularly natural science, in modern society, and the assumption that the methods of science are necessarily applicable to every subject matter. So their aim is not to attack science but to put it in place – to show that science is simply one among equals, and to free other disciplines from the tyranny that science supposedly exerts over them.

Scientism is obviously quite a vague doctrine, and since the term is in effect one of abuse, almost nobody would admit to believing it. Nonetheless, something quite like science-worship is a genuine feature of the intellectual landscape. This is not necessarily a bad thing – perhaps science deserves to be worshipped. But it is certainly a real phenomenon. One field that is often accused of science-worship is contemporary Anglo-American philosophy (of which philosophy of science is just one branch). Traditionally, philosophy is regarded as a humanities subject, despite its close historical links to mathematics and science, and with good reason. For the questions that philosophy addresses include the nature of knowledge, of morality, of rationality, of human well-being, and more, none of which appear soluble by scientific methods. No branch of science tells us how we should lead our lives, what knowledge is, or what human happiness involves; these are quintessentially philosophical questions.

Despite the apparent impossibility of answering philosophical questions through science, quite a few contemporary philosophers do believe that science is the only legitimate path to knowledge. Questions that cannot be resolved by scientific means are not genuine questions at all, they hold. This view is often associated with the late Willard van Orman Quine, arguably the most important American philosopher of the 20th century. The grounds for the view lie in a doctrine called 'naturalism', which stresses that we human beings are part and parcel of the natural world, not something apart from it, as was once believed. Since science studies the whole of the natural world, surely it should be capable of revealing the complete truth about the human condition, leaving nothing left for philosophy? Adherents of this view sometimes add that science undeniably makes progress, while philosophy seems to discuss the same questions for centuries on end. On this conception, there is no such thing as distinctively philosophical knowledge, for all knowledge is scientific knowledge. In so far as there is a role for philosophy at all, it consists in 'clarifying scientific concepts' – clearing the brush so that scientists can get on with their work.

Not surprisingly, many philosophers reject this subordination of their discipline to science; this is one of the main sources of opposition to scientism. They argue that philosophical enquiry reveals truths about a realm that science cannot touch. Philosophical questions are incapable of being resolved by scientific means, but are none the worse for that: science is not the only path to the truth. Proponents of this view can allow that philosophy should aim to be *consistent* with the sciences, in the sense of not advancing claims that conflict with what science teaches us. And they can allow that the sciences deserve to be treated with great respect. What they reject is scientific imperialism – the idea that science is capable of answering all the important questions about man and his place in nature. Advocates of this position usually think of themselves as naturalists too. They do not normally hold that we humans are somehow outside the natural order, and so exempt from the scope of science. They allow that we are just another biological species, and that our bodies are ultimately composed of physical particles, like everything else in the universe. But they deny that this implies that scientific methods are appropriate for addressing every question of interest.

A similar issue arises regarding the relation between the natural sciences and the social sciences. Just as philosophers sometimes complain of 'science worship' in their discipline, so social scientists sometimes complain of 'natural science worship' in theirs. There is no denying that the natural sciences – physics, chemistry, biology, etc. – are in a more advanced state than the social sciences – economics, sociology, anthropology, etc. A number of people have wondered why this is so. It can hardly be because natural scientists are smarter than social scientists. One possible answer is that the *methods* of the natural sciences are superior to those of the social sciences. If this is correct, then what the social sciences need to do to catch up is to ape the methods of the natural sciences. And to some extent, this has actually happened. The increasing use of mathematics in the social sciences may be partly a result of this attitude. Physics made a great leap forward when Galileo took the step of applying mathematical language to the description of motion; so it is tempting to think that a comparable leap forward might be achievable in the social sciences, if a comparable way of 'mathematicizing' their subject matter can be found.

However, some social scientists strongly resist the suggestion that they should look up to the natural sciences in this way, just as some philosophers strongly resist the idea that they should look up to science as a whole. They argue that the methods of natural science are not necessarily appropriate for studying social phenomena. Why should the very same techniques that are useful in astronomy, for example, be equally useful for studying societies? Those who hold this view deny that the more advanced state of the natural sciences is attributable to the distinctive methods of enquiry they employ, and thus see no reason to extend those methods to the social sciences. They often point out that the social sciences are younger than the natural sciences, and that the complex nature of social phenomena makes successful social science very hard to do.

Neither the scientism issue nor the parallel issue about natural and social science is easy to resolve. In part, this is because it is far from clear what exactly the 'methods of science', or the 'methods of natural science', actually comprise – a point that is often overlooked by both sides in the debate. If we want to know whether the methods of science are applicable to every subject matter, or whether they are capable of answering every important question, we obviously need to know what exactly those methods *are*. But as we have seen in previous chapters, this is much less straightforward a question than it seems. Certainly we know some of the main features of scientific enquiry: induction, experimental testing, observation, theory construction, inference to the best explanation, and so on. But this list does not provide a precise definition of 'the scientific method'. Nor is it obvious that such a definition *could* be provided. Science changes greatly over time, so the assumption that there is a fixed, unchanging 'scientific method', used by all scientific disciplines at all times, is far from inevitable. But this assumption is implicit both in the claim that science is the one true path to knowledge *and* in the counter-claim that some questions cannot be answered by scientific methods. This suggests that, to some extent at least, the debate about scientism may rest on a false presupposition.

Science and religion

The tension between science and religion is old and well documented. Perhaps the best-known example is Galileo's clash with the Catholic Church. In 1633 the Inquisition forced Galileo to publicly recant his Copernican views, and condemned him to spend the last years of his life under house arrest in Florence. The Church objected to the Copernican theory because it contravened the Holy Scriptures, of course. In recent times, the most prominent science/religion clash has been the bitter dispute between Darwinists and creationists in the United States, which will be our focus here.

Theological opposition to Darwin's theory of evolution is nothing new. When the *Origin of Species* was published in 1859, it immediately attracted criticism from churchmen in England. The reason is obvious: Darwin's theory maintains that all current species, including humans, have descended from common ancestors over a long period of time. This theory clearly contradicts the Book of Genesis, which says that God created all living creatures over a period of six days. So the choice looks stark: either you believe Darwin or you believe the Bible, but not both. Nonetheless, many committed Darwinians have found ways to reconcile their Christian faith with their belief in evolution – including a number of eminent biologists. One way is simply not to think about the clash too much. Another, more intellectually honest way is to argue that the Book of Genesis should not be interpreted literally – it should be regarded as allegorical, or symbolic. For after all, Darwin's theory is quite compatible with the existence of God, and with many other tenets of Christianity. It is only the literal truth of the biblical story of creation that Darwinism rules out. So a suitably attenuated version of Christianity can be rendered compatible with Darwinism.

However, in the United States, particularly in the Southern states, many evangelical Protestants have been unwilling to bend their religious beliefs to fit scientific findings. They insist that the biblical account of creation is literally true, and that Darwin's theory of evolution is therefore completely wrong. This opinion is known as 'creationism', and is accepted by some 40% of the adult population in the US, a far greater proportion than in Britain and Europe. Creationism is a powerful political force, and has had considerable influence on the teaching of biology in American schools, much to the dismay of scientists. In the famous 'monkey trial' of the 1920s, a Tennessee school teacher was convicted of teaching evolution to his pupils, in violation of state law. (The law was finally overturned by the Supreme Court in 1967.) In part because of the monkey trial, the subject of evolution was omitted altogether from the biology curriculum in US high schools for many decades. Generations of American adults grew up knowing nothing of Darwin.

This situation began to change in the 1960s, sparking a fresh round of battles between creationists and Darwinists, and giving rise to the movement called 'creation science'. Creationists want high-school students to learn the biblical story of creation, exactly as it appears in the Book of Genesis. But the American constitution prohibits the teaching of religion in public schools. The concept of creation science was designed to circumvent this. Its inventors argued that the biblical account of creation provides a better scientific explanation of life on earth than Darwin's theory of evolution. So teaching biblical creation does not violate the constitutional ban, for it counts as science, not religion! Across the Deep South, demands were made for creation science to be taught in biology classes, and they were very often heeded. In 1981 the state of Arkansas passed a law calling for biology teachers to give 'equal time' to evolution and to creation science, and other states followed suit. Though the Arkansas law was ruled unconstitutional by a federal judge in 1982, the call for 'equal time' continues to be heard today. It is often presented as a fair compromise – faced with two conflicting sets of beliefs, what could be fairer than giving equal time to each? Opinion polls show that an overwhelming majority of American adults agree: they want creation science to be taught alongside evolution in the public schools.

However, virtually all professional biologists regard creation science as a sham – a dishonest and misguided attempt to promote religious beliefs under the guise of science, with extremely harmful educational consequences. To counter this opposition, creation scientists have put great effort into trying to undermine Darwinism. They argue that the evidence for Darwinism is very inconclusive, so Darwinism is not established fact but rather just a theory. In addition, they have focused on various internal disputes among Darwinians, and picked on a few incautious remarks by individual biologists, in an attempt to show that disagreeing with the theory of evolution is scientifically respectable. They conclude that since Darwinism is 'just a theory', students should be exposed to alternative theories too – such as the creationist one that God made the world in six days.

In a way, the creationists are perfectly correct that Darwinism is 'just a theory' and not proven fact. As we saw in Chapter 2, it is never possible to *prove* that a scientific theory is true, in the strict sense of proof, for the inference from data to theory is invariably non-deductive. But this is a general point – it has nothing to do with the theory of evolution *per se*. By the same token, we could argue that it is 'just a theory' that the earth goes round the sun, or that water is made of H_2O, or that unsupported objects tend to fall, so students should be presented with alternatives to each of these. But creation scientists do not argue this. They are not sceptical about science as a whole, but about the theory of evolution in particular. So if their position is to be defensible, it cannot simply turn on the point that our data doesn't guarantee the truth of Darwin's theory. For the same is true of every scientific theory, and indeed of most common-sense beliefs too.

To be fair to the creation scientists, they do offer arguments that are specific to the theory of evolution. One of their favourite arguments is that the fossil record is extremely patchy, particularly when it comes to the supposed ancestors of *Homo sapiens*. There is some truth in this charge. Evolutionists have long puzzled over the gaps in the fossil record. One persistent puzzle is why there are so few 'transition fossils' – fossils of creatures intermediate between two species. If later species evolved from earlier ones as Darwin's theory asserts, surely we would expect transition fossils to be very common? Creationists take puzzles of this sort to show that Darwin's theory is just wrong. But the creationist arguments are uncompelling, notwithstanding the real difficulties in understanding the fossil record. For fossils are not the only or even the main source of evidence for the theory of evolution, as creationists would know if they had read *The Origin of Species*. Comparative anatomy is another important source of evidence, as are embryology, biogeography, and genetics. Consider, for example, the fact that humans and chimpanzees share 98% of their DNA. This and thousands of similar facts make perfect sense if the theory of evolution is true, and thus constitute excellent evidence for the theory. Of course, creation scientists can explain such facts too. They can claim that God decided to make humans and chimpanzees genetically similar, for reasons of His own. But the possibility of giving 'explanations' of this sort really just points to the fact that Darwin's theory is not logically entailed by the data. As we have seen, the same is true of every scientific theory. The creationists have merely highlighted the general methodological point that data can always be explained in a multitude of ways. This point is true, but shows nothing special about Darwinism.

Though the arguments of the creation scientists are uniformly unsound, the creationist/Darwinist controversy does raise important questions concerning science education. How should the clash between science and faith be dealt with in a secular education system? Who should determine the content of high-school science classes? Should tax payers have a say in what gets taught in the schools they pay for? Should parents who don't want their children to be taught about evolution, or some other scientific matter, be overruled by the state? Public policy matters such as these normally receive little discussion, but the clash between Darwinists and creationists has brought them to prominence.

Is science value free?

Almost everybody would agree that scientific knowledge has sometimes been used for unethical ends – in the manufacture of nuclear, biological, and chemical weapons, for example. But cases such as these do not show that there is something ethically objectionable about scientific knowledge itself. It is the *use* to which that knowledge is put that is unethical. Indeed, many philosophers would say that it makes no sense to talk about science or scientific knowledge being ethical or unethical *per se*. For science is concerned with facts, and facts in themselves have no ethical significance. It is what we do with those facts that is right or wrong, moral or immoral. According to this view, science is essentially a *value-free* activity – its job is just to provide information about the world. What society chooses to do with that information is another matter.

Not all philosophers accept this picture of science as neutral with respect to matters of value, nor the underlying fact/value dichotomy on which it rests. Some argue that the ideal of value-neutrality is unattainable – scientific enquiry is invariably laden with value judgements. (This is analogous to the claim that all observation is theory-laden, discussed in Chapter 4. Indeed, the two claims are often found hand-in-hand.) One argument against the possibility of value-free science stems from the obvious fact that scientists have to choose what to study – not everything can be examined at once. So judgements about the relative importance of different possible objects of study will have to be made, and these are value judgements, in a weak sense. Another argument stems from the fact, with which you should now be familiar, that any set of data can in principle be explained in more than one way. A scientist's choice of theory will thus never be uniquely determined by his data. Some philosophers take this to show that values are inevitably involved in theory choice, and thus that science cannot possibly be value-free. A third argument is that scientific knowledge cannot be divorced from its intended applications in the way that value-neutrality would require. On this view, it is naïve to picture scientists as disinterestedly doing research for its own sake, without a thought for its practical applications. The fact that much scientific research today is funded by private enterprises, who obviously have vested commercial interests, lends some credence to this view.

Though interesting, these arguments are all somewhat abstract – they seek to show that science could not be value free as a matter of principle, rather than identifying actual cases of values intruding in science. But specific accusations of value-ladenness have also been made. One such case concerns the discipline called human sociobiology, which generated considerable controversy in the 1970s and 1980s. Human sociobiology is the attempt to apply principles of Darwinian theory to human behaviour. At first blush this project sounds perfectly reasonable. For humans are just another species of animal, and biologists agree that Darwinian theory can explain a lot of animal behaviour. For example, there is an obvious Darwinian explanation for why mice usually run away when they see cats. In the past, mice that did not behave this way tended to leave fewer offspring than ones that did, for they got eaten; assuming that the behaviour was genetically based, and thus transmitted from parents to offspring, over a number of generations it would have spread through the population. This explains why mice today run away from cats. Explanations of this sort are known as 'Darwinian' or 'adaptationist' explanations.

Human sociobiologists (henceforth simply 'sociobiologists') believe that many behavioural traits in humans can be given adaptationist explanations. One of their favourite examples is incest-avoidance. Incest – or sexual relations between members of the same family – is regarded as taboo in virtually every human society, and subject to legal and moral sanctions in most. This fact is quite striking, given that sexual mores are otherwise quite diverse across human societies. Why the prohibition on incest? Sociobiologists offer the following explanation. Children born of incestuous relationships often have serious genetic defects. So in the past, those who practised incest would have tended to leave fewer viable offspring than those who didn't. Assuming that the incest-avoiding behaviour was genetically based, and thus transmitted from parents to their offspring, over a number of generations it would have spread through the population. This explains why incest is so rarely found in human societies today.

Understandably enough, many people feel uneasy with this sort of explanation. For, in effect, sociobiologists are saying that we are genetically pre-programmed to avoid incest. This conflicts with the common-sense view that we avoid incest because we have been taught that it is wrong, i.e. that our behaviour has a cultural rather than a biological explanation. And incest-avoidance is actually one of the least controversial examples. Other behaviours for which sociobiologists offer adaptationist explanations include rape, aggression, xenophobia, and male promiscuity. In each case, their argument is the same: individuals who engaged in the behaviour out-reproduced individuals who didn't, and the behaviour was genetically based, hence transmitted from parents to their offspring. Of course, not all humans are aggressive, xenophobic, or engage in rape. But this does not show that the sociobiologists are wrong. For their argument only requires that these behaviours have a genetic component, i.e. that there is some gene or genes which increases the probability that its carriers will engage in the behaviours. This is much weaker than saying that the behaviours are totally genetically determined, which is almost certainly false. In other words, the sociobiological story is meant to explain why there is a *disposition* among humans to be aggressive, xenophobic, and to rape – even if such dispositions are infrequently manifested. So the fact that aggression, xenophobia, and rape are (thankfully) quite rare does not in itself prove the sociobiologists wrong.

Sociobiology attracted strong criticism from a wide range of scholars. Some of this was strictly scientific. Critics pointed out that sociobiological hypotheses were extremely hard to test, and should thus be viewed as interesting conjectures, not established truths. But others objected more fundamentally, claiming that the whole sociobiological research programme was ideologically suspect. They saw it as an attempt to justify or excuse anti-social behaviour, usually by men. By arguing that rape, for example, has a genetic component, sociobiologists were implying that it was 'natural' and thus that rapists were not really responsible for their actions – they were simply obeying their genetic impulses. 'How can we blame rapists, if their genes are responsible for their behaviour?', the sociobiologists seemed to be saying. Sociobiological explanations of xenophobia and male promiscuity were regarded as equally pernicious. They seemed to imply that phenomena such as racism and marital infidelity, which most people regard as undesirable, were natural and inevitable – the product of our genetic heritage. In short, critics charged that sociobiology was a value-laden science, and the values it was laden with were very dubious. Perhaps unsurprisingly, these critics included many feminists and social scientists.

One possible response to this charge is to insist on the distinction between facts and values. Take the case of rape. Presumably, either there is a gene which disposes men to rape and which spread by natural selection, or there is not. It is a question of pure scientific fact, though not an easy one to answer. But facts are one thing, values another. Even if there is such a gene, that does not make rape excusable or acceptable. Nor does it make rapists any the less responsible for their actions, for nobody thinks such a gene would literally *force* men to rape. At most, the gene might predispose men to rape, but innate predispositions can be overcome by cultural training, and everybody is taught that rape is wrong. The same applies to xenophobia, aggression, and promiscuity. Even if sociobiological explanations of these behaviours are correct, this has no implications for how we should run society, or for any other political or ethical matters. Ethics cannot be deduced from science. So there is nothing ideologically suspect about sociobiology. Like all sciences, it is simply trying to tell us the facts about the world. Sometimes the facts are disturbing, but we must learn to live with them.

If this response is correct, it means we should sharply distinguish the 'scientific' objections to sociobiology from the 'ideological' objections. Reasonable though this sounds, there is one point it doesn't address: advocates of sociobiology have tended to be politically right-wing, while its critics have tended to come from the political left. There are many exceptions to this generalization, especially to the first half of it, but few would deny the trend altogether. If sociobiology is simply an impartial enquiry into the facts, what explains the trend? Why should there be any correlation at all between political opinions and attitudes towards sociobiology? This is a tricky question to answer. For though some sociobiologists may have had hidden political agendas, and though some of sociobiology's critics have had opposing agendas of their own, the correlation extends even to those who debate the issue in apparently scientific terms. This suggests, though does not prove, that the 'ideological' and 'scientific' issues may not be quite so easy to separate after all. So the question of whether sociobiology is a value-free science is less easy to answer than might have been supposed.

To conclude, it is inevitable that an enterprise such as science, which occupies so pivotal a role in modern society and commands so much public money, should find itself subject to criticism from a variety of sources. It is also a good thing, for uncritical acceptance of everything that scientists say and do would be both unhealthy and dogmatic. It is safe to predict that science in the 21st century, through its technological applications, will impact on everyday life to an even greater extent than it has already. So the question 'is science a good thing?' will become yet more pressing. Philosophical reflection may not produce a final, unequivocal answer to this question, but it can help to isolate the key issues and encourage a rational, balanced discussion of them.

Further reading

Chapter 1
A. Rupert Hall, *The Revolution in Science 1500–1750* (Longman, 1983)
contains a good account of the scientific revolution. Detailed treatment
of particular topics in the history of science can be found in R. C. Olby,
G. N. Cantor, J. R. R. Christie, and M. J. S. Hodge (eds.), *Companion to
the History of Modern Science* (Routledge, 1990). There are many good
introductions to philosophy of science. Two recent ones include
Alexander Rosenberg, *The Philosophy of Science* (Routledge, 2000) and
Barry Gower, *Scientific Method* (Routledge, 1997). Martin Curd and
J. A. Cover (eds.), *Philosophy of Science: The Central Issues* (W.W.
Norton, 1998) contains readings on all the main issues in philosophy of
science, with extensive commentaries by the editors. Karl Popper's
attempt to demarcate science from pseudo-science can be found in his
Conjectures and Refutations (Routledge, 1963). A good discussion of
Popper's demarcation criterion is Donald Gillies, *Philosophy of Science
in the 20th Century* (Blackwell, Part IV, 1993). Anthony O'Hear, *Karl
Popper* (Routledge, 1980) is a general introduction to Popper's
philosophical views.

Chapter 2
Wesley Salmon, *The Foundations of Scientific Inference* (University of
Pittsburgh Press, 1967) contains a very clear discussion of all the issues
raised in this chapter. Hume's original argument can be found in Book
IV, section 4 of his *Enquiry Concerning Human Understanding*, ed.

L. A. Selby-Bigge (Clarendon Press, 1966). Strawson's article is in Richard Swinburne (ed.), *The Justification of Induction* (Oxford University Press, 1974); the other papers in this volume are also of interest. Gilbert Harman's paper on IBE is 'The Inference to the Best Explanation', *Philosophical Review* 1965 (74), pp. 88–95. Peter Lipton, *Inference to the Best Explanation* (Routledge, 1991), is a book-length treatment of the topic. Popper's attempted solution of the problem of induction is in *The Logic of Scientific Discovery* (Basic Books, 1959); the relevant section is reprinted in M. Curd and J. Cover (eds.), *Philosophy of Science* (W.W. Norton, 1998), pp. 426–32. A good critique of Popper is Wesley Salmon's 'Rational Prediction', also reprinted in Curd and Cover (eds.), pp. 433–44. The various interpretations of probability are discussed in Donald Gillies, *Philosophical Theories of Probability* (Routledge, 2000) and in Brian Skryms, *Choice and Chance* (Wadsworth, 1986).

Chapter 3

Hempel's original presentation of the covering law model can be found in his *Aspects of Scientific Explanation* (Free Press, 1965, essay 12). Wesley Salmon, *Four Decades of Scientific Explanation* (University of Minnesota Press, 1989) is a very useful account of the debate instigated by Hempel's work. Two collections of papers on scientific explanation are Joseph Pitt (ed.), *Theories of Explanation* (Oxford University Press, 1988) and David-Hillel Ruben (ed.), *Explanation* (Oxford University Press, 1993). The suggestion that consciousness can never be explained scientifically is defended by Colin McGinn, *Problems of Consciousness* (Blackwell, 1991); for discussion, see Martin Davies 'The Philosophy of Mind' in A. C. Grayling (ed.), *Philosophy: A Guide Through the Subject* (Oxford University Press, 1995) and Jaegwon Kim, *Philosophy of Mind* (Westview Press, 1993, chapter 7). The idea that multiple realization accounts for the autonomy of the higher-level sciences is developed in a difficult paper by Jerry Fodor, 'Special Sciences', *Synthese* 28, pp. 77–115. For more on the important topic of reductionism, see the papers in section 8 of M. Curd and J. Cover (eds.), *Philosophy of Science* (W.W. Norton, 1998) and the editors' commentary.

Chapter 4

Jarrett Leplin (ed.), *Scientific Realism* (University of California Press, 1984) is an important collection of papers on the realism/anti-realism debate. A recent book-length defence of realism is Stathis Psillos, *Scientific Realism: How Science Tracks Truth* (Routledge, 1999). Grover Maxwell's paper 'The Ontological Status of Theoretical Entities' is reprinted in M. Curd and J. Cover (eds.), *Philosophy of Science* (W.W. Norton, 1998), pp. 1052–63. Bas van Fraassen's very influential defence of anti-realism is in *The Scientific Image* (Oxford University Press, 1980). Critical discussions of van Fraassen's work, with replies by van Fraassen, can be found in C. Hooker and P. Churchland (eds.), *Images of Science* (University of Chicago Press, 1985). The argument that scientific realism conflicts with the historical record is developed by Larry Laudan in 'A Confutation of Convergent Realism', *Philosophy of Science* 1981 (48), pp. 19–48, reprinted in Leplin (ed.), *Scientific Realism*. The 'no miracles' argument was originally developed by Hilary Putnam; see his *Mathematics, Matter and Method* (Cambridge University Press, 1975), pp. 69ff. Larry Laudan's 'Demystifying Underdetermination' in M. Curd and J. Cover (eds.), *Philosophy of Science* (W.W. Norton, 1998), pp. 320–53, is a good discussion of the concept of underdetermination.

Chapter 5

Important papers by the original logical positivists can be found in H. Feigl and M. Brodbeck (eds.), *Readings in the Philosophy of Science* (Appleton-Century-Croft, 1953). Thomas Kuhn, *The Structure of Scientific Revolutions* (University of Chicago Press, 1963) is for the most part very readable; all post-1970 editions contain Kuhn's Postscript. Kuhn's later thoughts, and his reflections on the debate sparked by his book, can be found in 'Objectivity, Value Judgment and Theory Choice' in his *The Essential Tension* (University of Chicago Press, 1977), and *The Road Since Structure* (University of Chicago Press, 2000). Two recent book-length discussions of Kuhn's work are Paul Hoyningen-Heune, *Reconstructing Scientific Revolutions: Thomas Kuhn's Philosophy of Science* (University of Chicago Press, 1993) and Alexander Bird, *Thomas Kuhn* (Princeton University Press, 2001). Paul Horwich (ed.), *World Changes* (MIT Press, 1993) contains discussions of Kuhn's work by well-known historians and philosophers of science, with comments by Kuhn himself.

Chapter 6

The original debate between Leibniz and Newton consists of five papers by Leibniz and five replies by Samuel Clarke, Newton's spokesman. These are reprinted in H. Alexander (ed.), *The Leibniz-Clarke Correspondence* (Manchester University Press, 1956). Good discussions can be found in Nick Huggett (ed.), *Space from Zeno to Einstein* (MIT Press, 1999) and Christopher Ray, *Time, Space and Philosophy* (Routledge, 1991). Biological classification is discussed from a philosophical viewpoint by Elliott Sober, *Philosophy of Biology* (Westview Press, 1993, chapter 7). A very detailed account of the clash between pheneticists and cladists is given by David Hull, *Science as a Process* (University of Chicago Press, 1988). Also useful is Ernst Mayr, 'Biological Classification: Towards a Synthesis of Opposing Methodologies' in E. Sober (ed.), *Conceptual Issues in Evolutionary Biology*, 2nd edn. (MIT Press, 1994). Jerry Fodor, *The Modularity of Mind* (MIT Press, 1983) is quite difficult but well worth the effort. Good discussions of the modularity issue can be found in Kim Sterelny, *The Representational Theory of Mind* (Blackwell, 1990) and J. L. Garfield, 'Modularity', in S. Guttenplan (ed.), *A Companion to the Philosophy of Mind* (Blackwell, 1994).

Chapter 7

Tom Sorell, *Scientism* (Routledge, 1991) contains a detailed discussion of the concept of scientism. The issue of whether the methods of natural science are applicable to social science is discussed by Alexander Rosenberg, *Philosophy of Social Science* (Clarendon Press, 1988) and David Papineau, *For Science in the Social Sciences* (Macmillan, 1978). The creationist/Darwinist controversy is examined in detail by Philip Kitcher, *Abusing Science: The Case Against Creation* (MIT Press, 1982). A typical piece of creationist writing is Duane Gish, *Evolution? The Fossils Say No!* (Creation Life Publishers, 1979). Good general discussions of the issue of value-ladenness include Larry Laudan, *Science and Values* (University of California Press, 1984) and Helen

Longino, *Science as Social Knowledge: Values and Objectivity in Scientific Inquiry* (Princeton University Press, 1990). The controversy over sociobiology was instigated by Edward O. Wilson, *Sociobiology* (Harvard University Press, 1975); also relevant is his *On Human Nature* (Bantam Books, 1978). A detailed and fair examination of the controversy is given by Philip Kitcher, *Vaulting Ambition: Sociobiology and the Quest for Human Nature* (MIT Press, 1985).

Index

Expand your collection of
VERY SHORT INTRODUCTIONS

ANCIENT PHILOSOPHY
A Very Short Introduction
Julia Annas

The tradition of ancient philosophy is a long, rich and varied one, in which a constant note is that of discussion and argument. This book aims to introduce readers to some ancient debates and to get them to engage with the ancient developments of philosophical themes. Getting away from the presentation of ancient philosophy as a succession of Great Thinkers, the book aims to give readers a sense of the freshness and liveliness of ancient philosophy, and of its wide variety of themes and styles.

'Incisive, elegant, and full of the excitement of doing philosophy, Julia Annas's Short Introduction boldly steps outside of conventional chronological ways of organizing material about the Greeks and Romans to get right to the heart of the human problems that exercised them, problems ranging from the relation between reason and emotion to the objectivity of truth. I can't think of a better way to begin.'

Martha Nussbaum, University of Chicago

www.oup.co.uk/vsi/ancientphilosophy

PHILOSOPHY
A Very Short Introduction
Edward Craig

This lively and engaging book is the ideal introduction for anyone who has ever been puzzled by what philosophy is or what it is for.

Edward Craig argues that philosophy is not an activity from another planet: learning about it is just a matter of broadening and deepening what most of us do already. He shows that philosophy is no mere intellectual pastime: thinkers such as Plato, Buddhist writers, Descartes, Hobbes, Hume, Hegel, Darwin, Mill and de Beauvoir were responding to real needs and events – much of their work shapes our lives today, and many of their concerns are still ours.

'A vigorous and engaging introduction that speaks to the philosopher in everyone.'

John Cottingham, University of Reading

'addresses many of the central philosophical questions in an engaging and thought-provoking style . . . Edward Craig is already famous as the editor of the best long work on philosophy (the Routledge Encyclopedia); now he deserves to become even better known as the author of one of the best short ones.'

Nigel Warburton, The Open University

www.oup.co.uk/isbn/0-19-285421-6

CONTINENTAL PHILOSOPHY
A Very Short Introduction
Simon Critchley

Continental philosophy is a contested concept which cuts to the heart of the identity of philosophy and its relevance to matters of public concern and personal life. This book attempts to answer the question 'What is Continental philosophy?' by telling a story that began with Kant 200 years ago and includes discussions of major philosophers like Nietzsche, Husserl and Heidegger. At the core of the book is a plea to place philosophy at the centre of cultural life, and thus reawaken its ancient definition of the love of wisdom that makes life worth living.

> 'Antagonism and mutual misrepresentation between so-called analytical and continental philosophy have helped shape the course of every significant development in Western intellectual life since the 1960s – structuralism, post-structuralism, postmodernism, gender studies, etc. Simon Critchley has skilfully and sympathetically sketched continental lines of thought so that strangers to their detail may enter them systematically enough that their principle texts begin to illuminate one another. It is a remarkable achievement.'
>
> **Stanley Cavell, Harvard University**

www.oup.co.uk/isbn/0-19-285359-7

Visit the
VERY SHORT INTRODUCTIONS
Web site

www.oup.co.uk/vsi

➤ **Information** about all published titles

➤ News of **forthcoming books**

➤ **Extracts** from the books, including titles not yet published

➤ **Reviews** and views

➤ **Links** to other **web sites** and main OUP web page

➤ Information about **VSIs in translation**

➤ **Contact** the editors

➤ **Order** other **VSIs** on-line